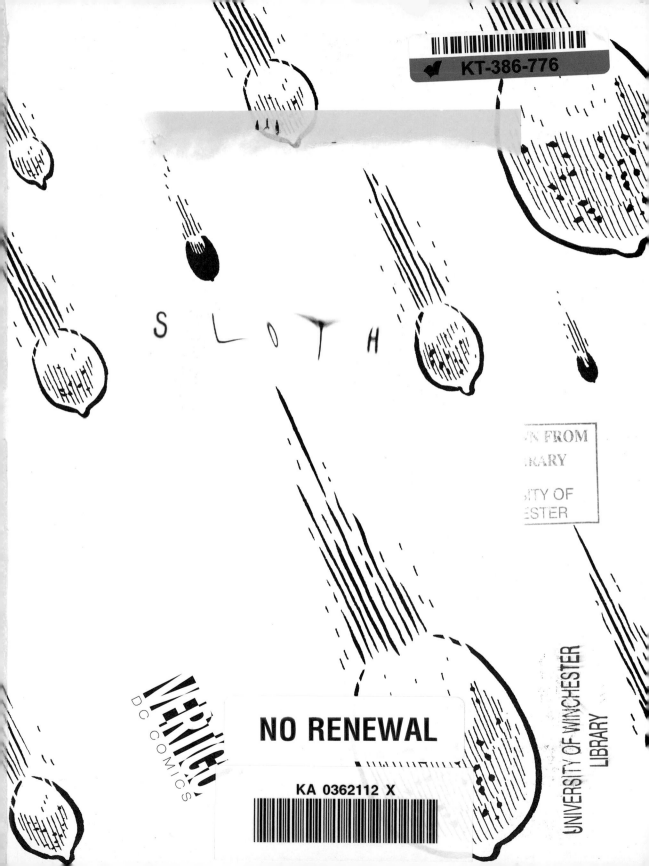

S L O T H

VERTIGO
DC COMICS

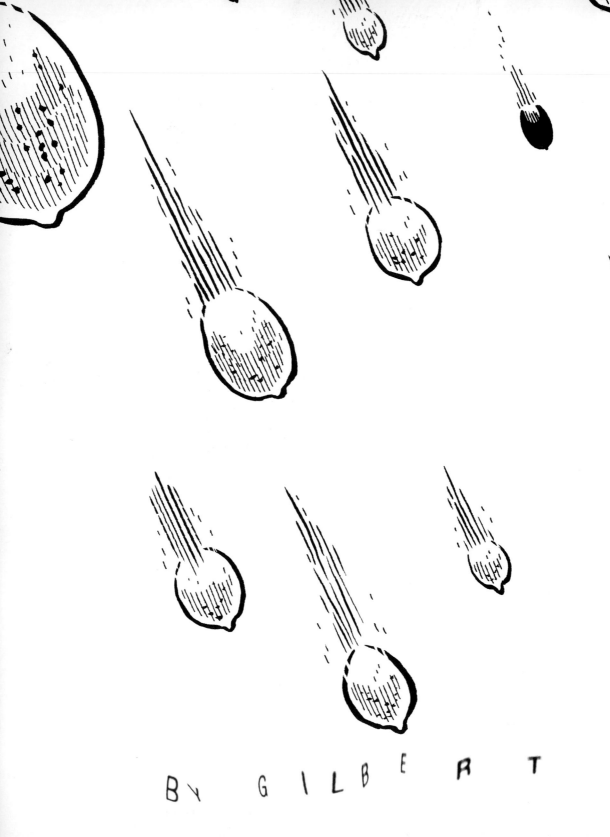

BY GILBERT

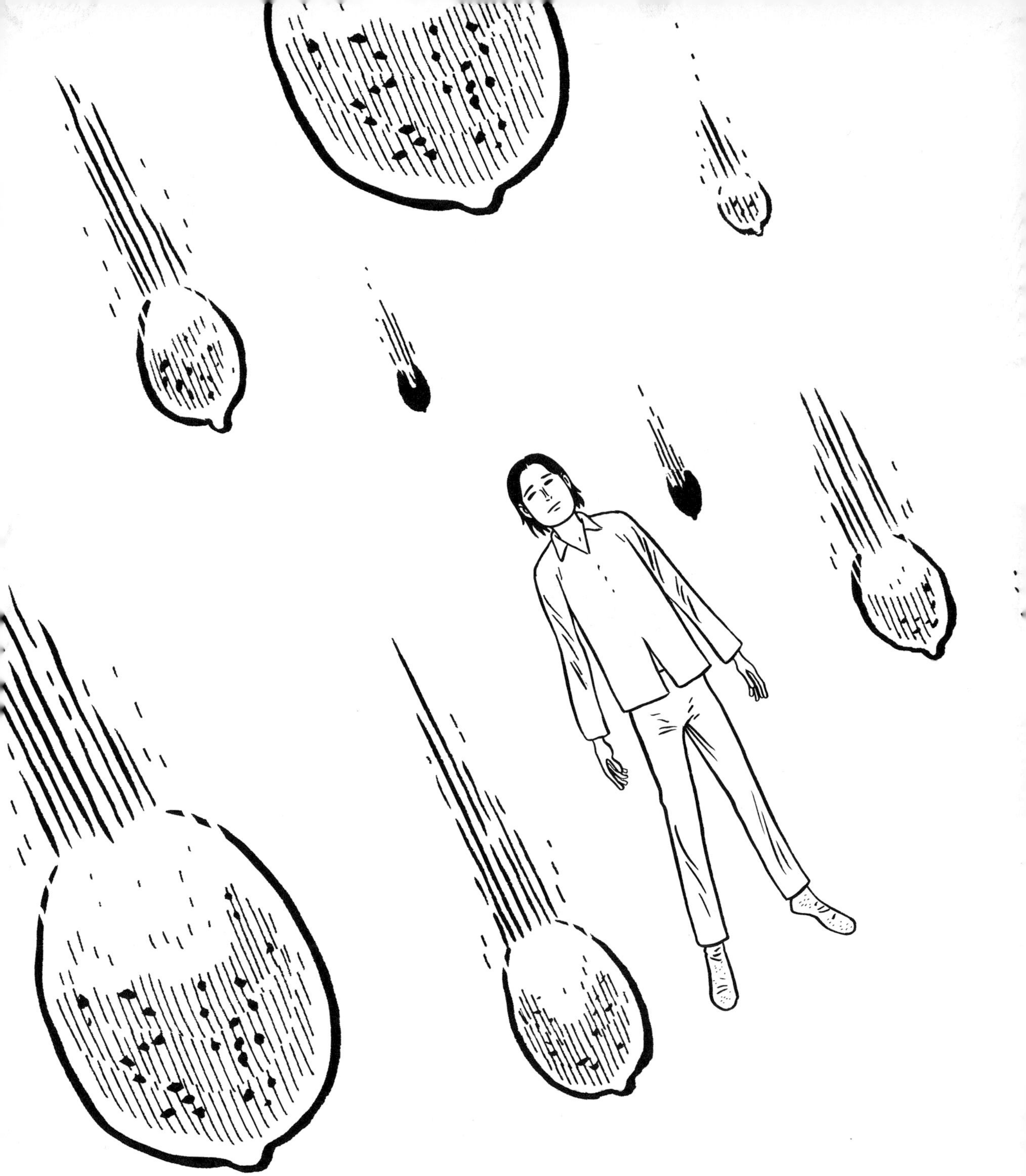

HERNANDEZ

LETTERING BY JARED K. FLETCHER

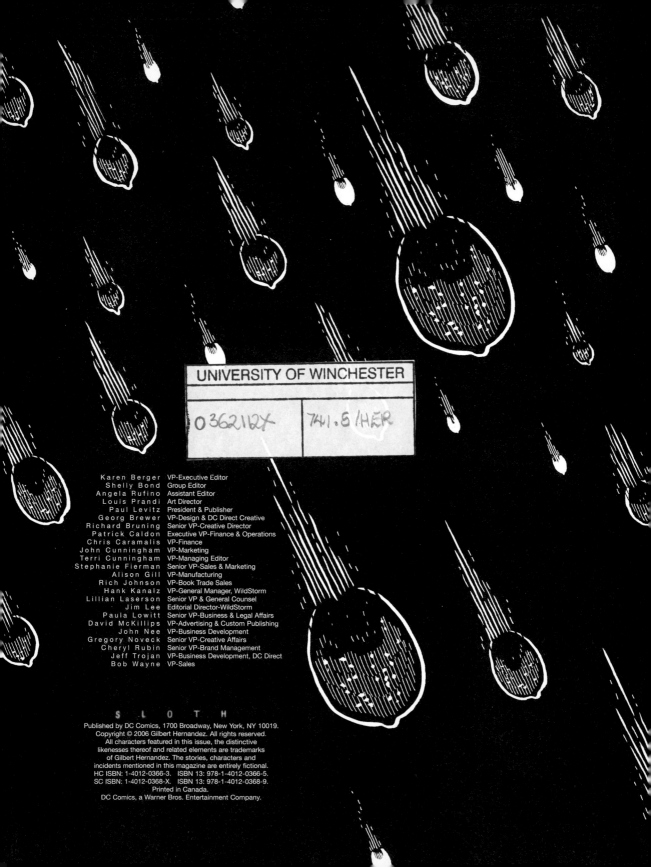

Karen Berger   VP-Executive Editor
Shelly Bond   Group Editor
Angela Rufino   Assistant Editor
Louis Prandi   Art Director
Paul Levitz   President & Publisher
Georg Brewer   VP-Design & DC Direct Creative
Richard Bruning   Senior VP-Creative Director
Patrick Caldon   Executive VP-Finance & Operations
Chris Caramalis   VP-Finance
John Cunningham   VP-Marketing
Terri Cunningham   VP-Managing Editor
Stephanie Fierman   Senior VP-Sales & Marketing
Alison Gill   VP-Manufacturing
Rich Johnson   VP-Book Trade Sales
Hank Kanalz   VP-General Manager, WildStorm
Lillian Laserson   Senior VP & General Counsel
Jim Lee   Editorial Director-WildStorm
Paula Lowitt   Senior VP-Business & Legal Affairs
David McKillips   VP-Advertising & Custom Publishing
John Nee   VP-Business Development
Gregory Noveck   Senior VP-Creative Affairs
Cheryl Rubin   Senior VP-Brand Management
Jeff Trojan   VP-Business Development, DC Direct
Bob Wayne   VP-Sales

S L O T H

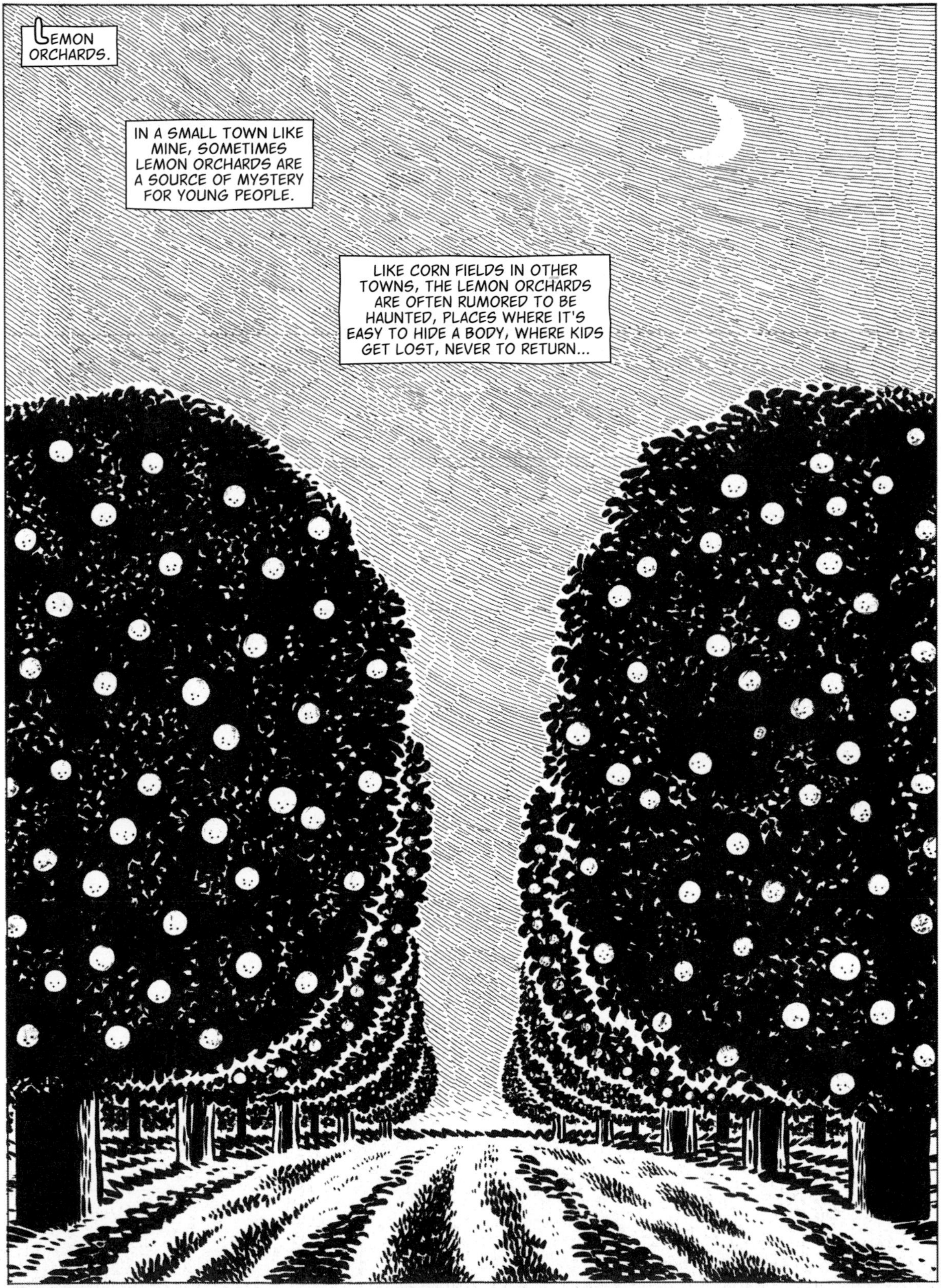
LEMON ORCHARDS.
IN A SMALL TOWN LIKE MINE, SOMETIMES LEMON ORCHARDS ARE A SOURCE OF MYSTERY FOR YOUNG PEOPLE.
LIKE CORN FIELDS IN OTHER TOWNS, THE LEMON ORCHARDS ARE OFTEN RUMORED TO BE HAUNTED, PLACES WHERE IT'S EASY TO HIDE A BODY, WHERE KIDS GET LOST, NEVER TO RETURN...

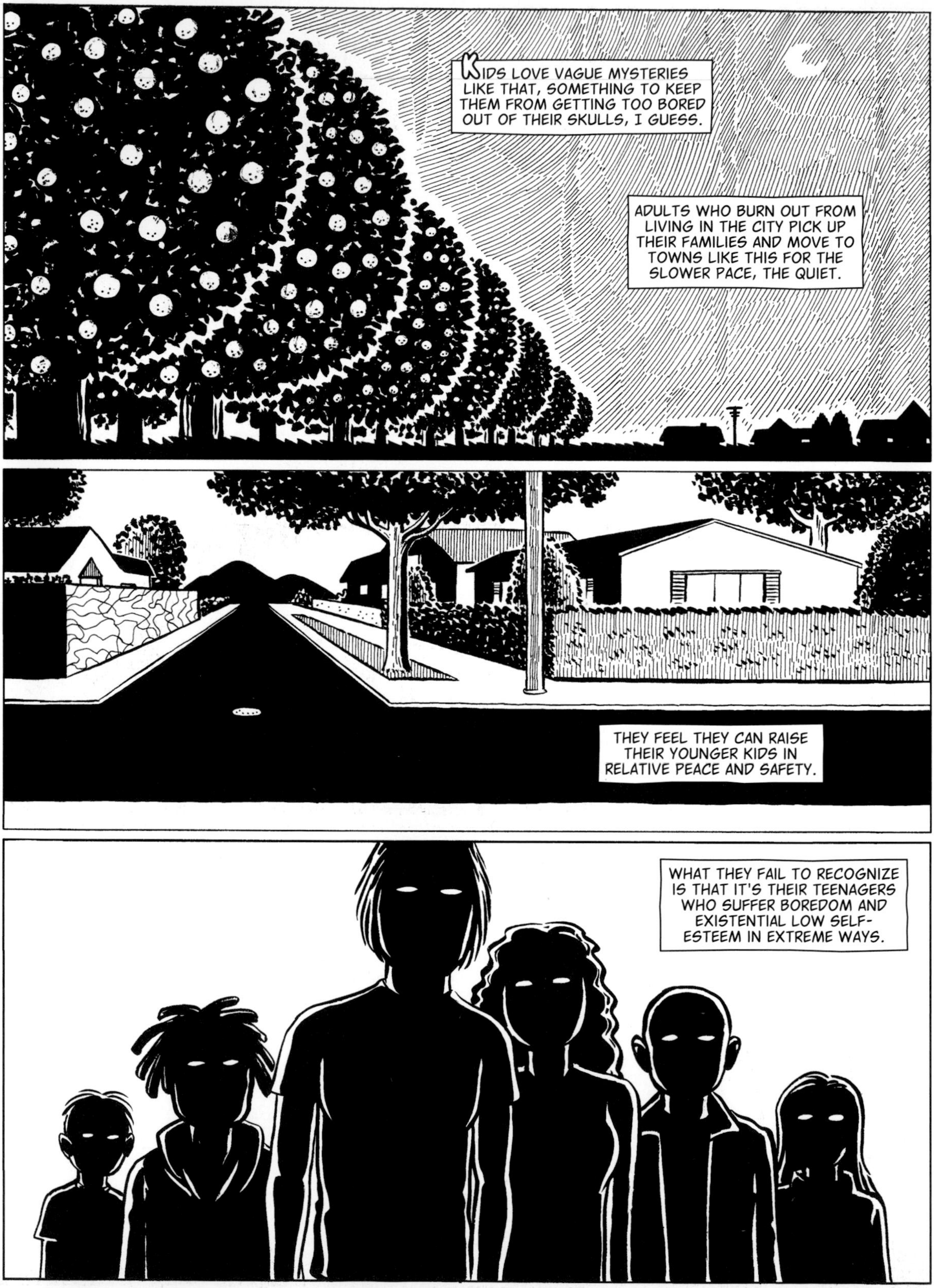
KIDS LOVE VAGUE MYSTERIES LIKE THAT, SOMETHING TO KEEP THEM FROM GETTING TOO BORED OUT OF THEIR SKULLS, I GUESS.
ADULTS WHO BURN OUT FROM LIVING IN THE CITY PICK UP THEIR FAMILIES AND MOVE TO TOWNS LIKE THIS FOR THE SLOWER PACE, THE QUIET.
THEY FEEL THEY CAN RAISE THEIR YOUNGER KIDS IN RELATIVE PEACE AND SAFETY.
WHAT THEY FAIL TO RECOGNIZE IS THAT IT'S THEIR TEENAGERS WHO SUFFER BOREDOM AND EXISTENTIAL LOW SELF-ESTEEM IN EXTREME WAYS.

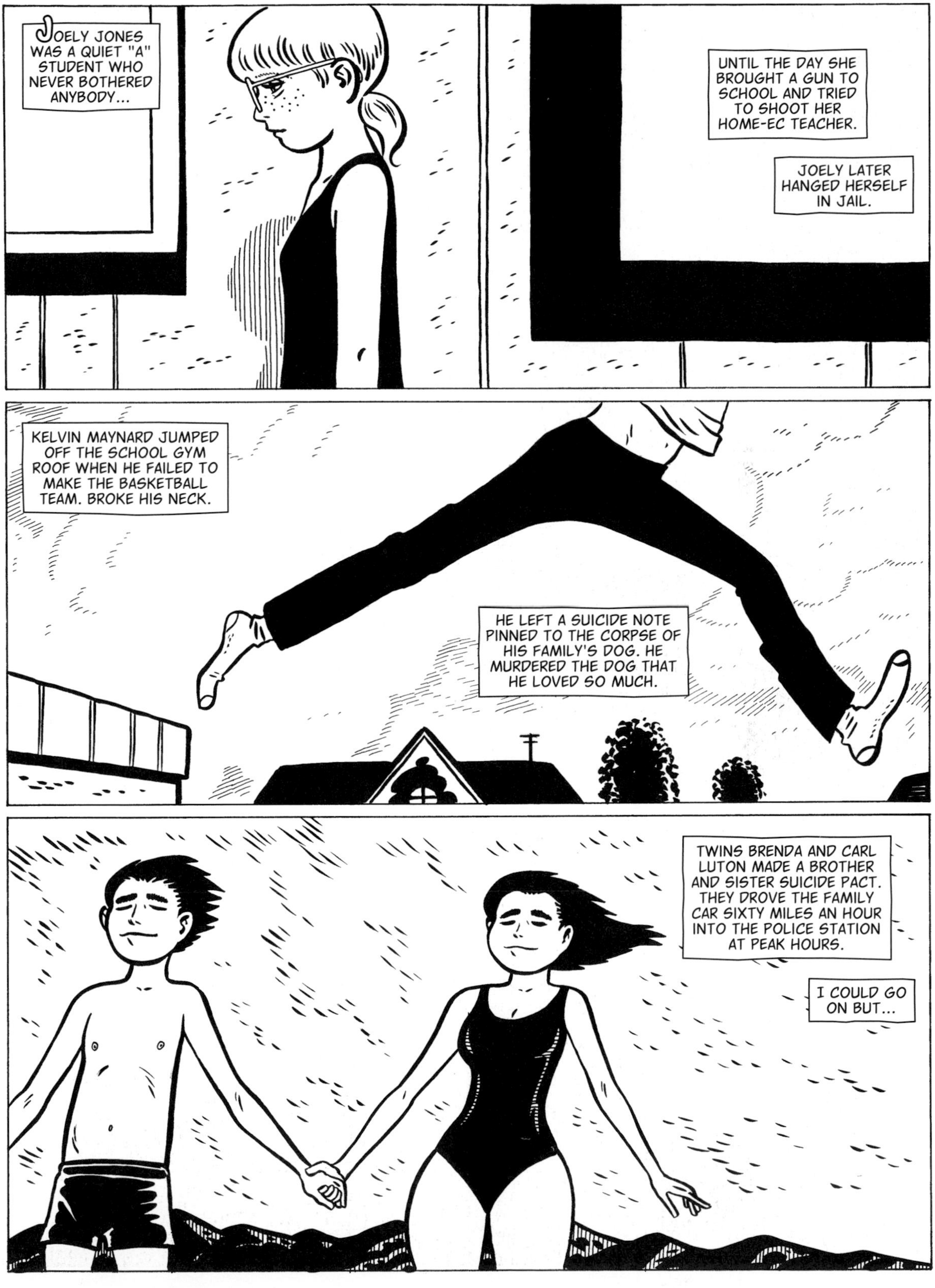
JOELY JONES WAS A QUIET "A" STUDENT WHO NEVER BOTHERED ANYBODY...
UNTIL THE DAY SHE BROUGHT A GUN TO SCHOOL AND TRIED TO SHOOT HER HOME-EC TEACHER.
JOELY LATER HANGED HERSELF IN JAIL.
KELVIN MAYNARD JUMPED OFF THE SCHOOL GYM ROOF WHEN HE FAILED TO MAKE THE BASKETBALL TEAM. BROKE HIS NECK.
HE LEFT A SUICIDE NOTE PINNED TO THE CORPSE OF HIS FAMILY'S DOG. HE MURDERED THE DOG THAT HE LOVED SO MUCH.
TWINS BRENDA AND CARL LUTON MADE A BROTHER AND SISTER SUICIDE PACT. THEY DROVE THE FAMILY CAR SIXTY MILES AN HOUR INTO THE POLICE STATION AT PEAK HOURS.
I COULD GO ON BUT...

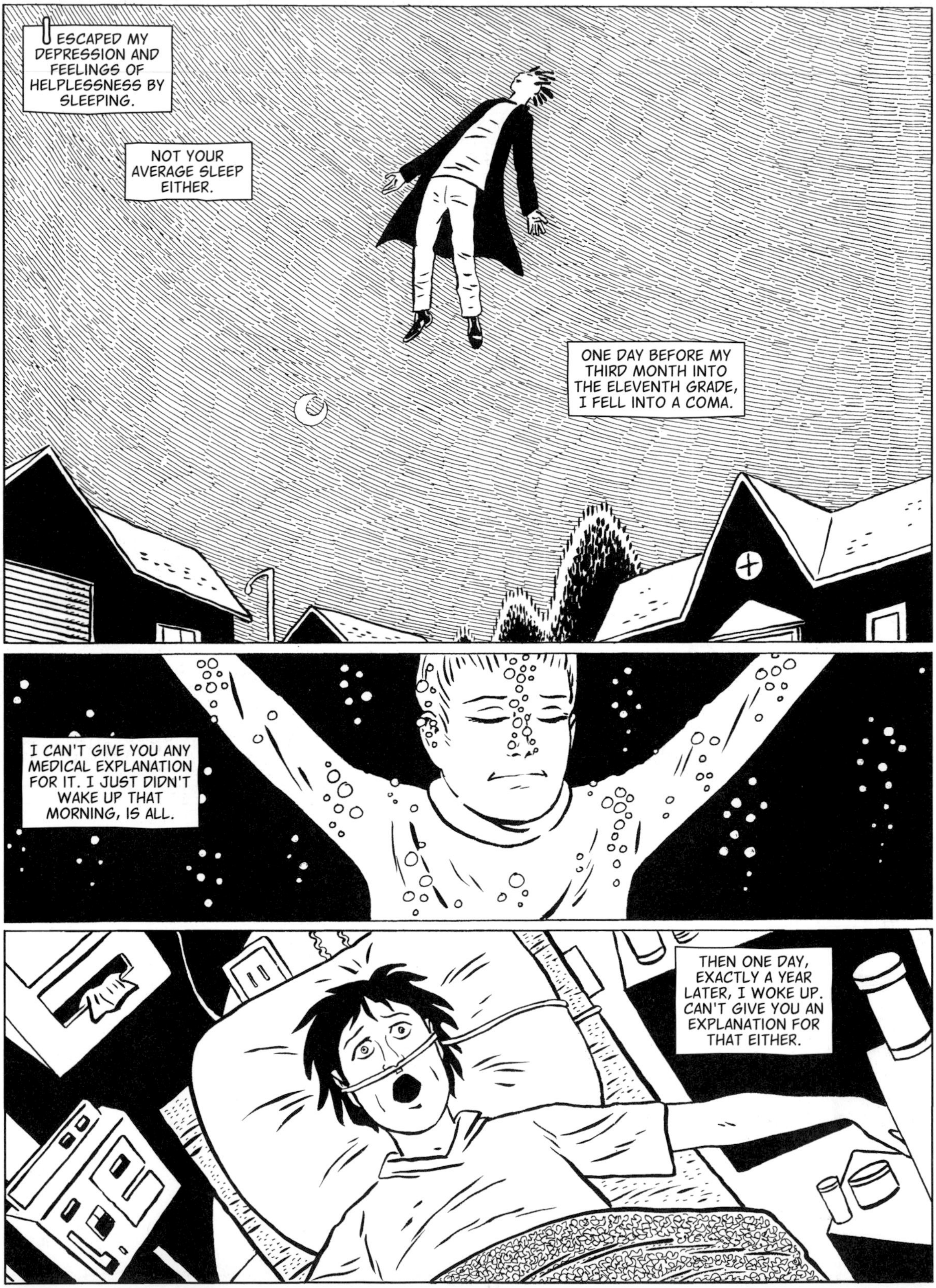
I ESCAPED MY DEPRESSION AND FEELINGS OF HELPLESSNESS BY SLEEPING.
NOT YOUR AVERAGE SLEEP EITHER.
ONE DAY BEFORE MY THIRD MONTH INTO THE ELEVENTH GRADE, I FELL INTO A COMA.
I CAN'T GIVE YOU ANY MEDICAL EXPLANATION FOR IT. I JUST DIDN'T WAKE UP THAT MORNING, IS ALL.
THEN ONE DAY, EXACTLY A YEAR LATER, I WOKE UP. CAN'T GIVE YOU AN EXPLANATION FOR THAT EITHER.

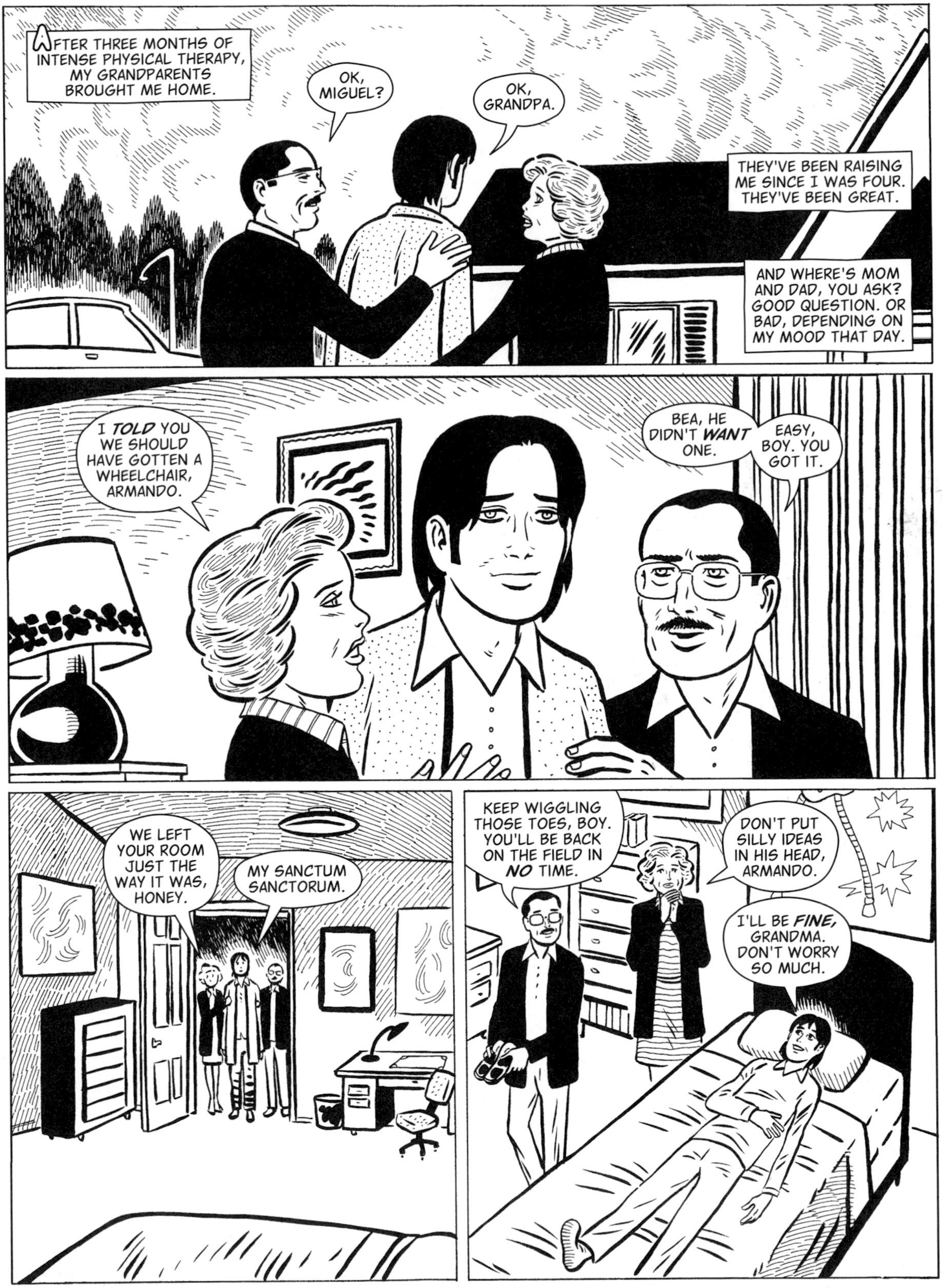
AFTER THREE MONTHS OF INTENSE PHYSICAL THERAPY, MY GRANDPARENTS BROUGHT ME HOME.
OK, MIGUEL?
OK, GRANDPA.
THEY'VE BEEN RAISING ME SINCE I WAS FOUR. THEY'VE BEEN GREAT.
AND WHERE'S MOM AND DAD, YOU ASK? GOOD QUESTION. OR BAD, DEPENDING ON MY MOOD THAT DAY.
I *TOLD* YOU WE SHOULD HAVE GOTTEN A WHEELCHAIR, ARMANDO.
BEA, HE DIDN'T *WANT* ONE.
EASY, BOY. YOU GOT IT.
WE LEFT YOUR ROOM JUST THE WAY IT WAS, HONEY.
MY SANCTUM SANCTORUM.
KEEP WIGGLING THOSE TOES, BOY. YOU'LL BE BACK ON THE FIELD IN *NO* TIME.
DON'T PUT SILLY IDEAS IN HIS HEAD, ARMANDO.
I'LL BE *FINE,* GRANDMA. DON'T WORRY SO MUCH.

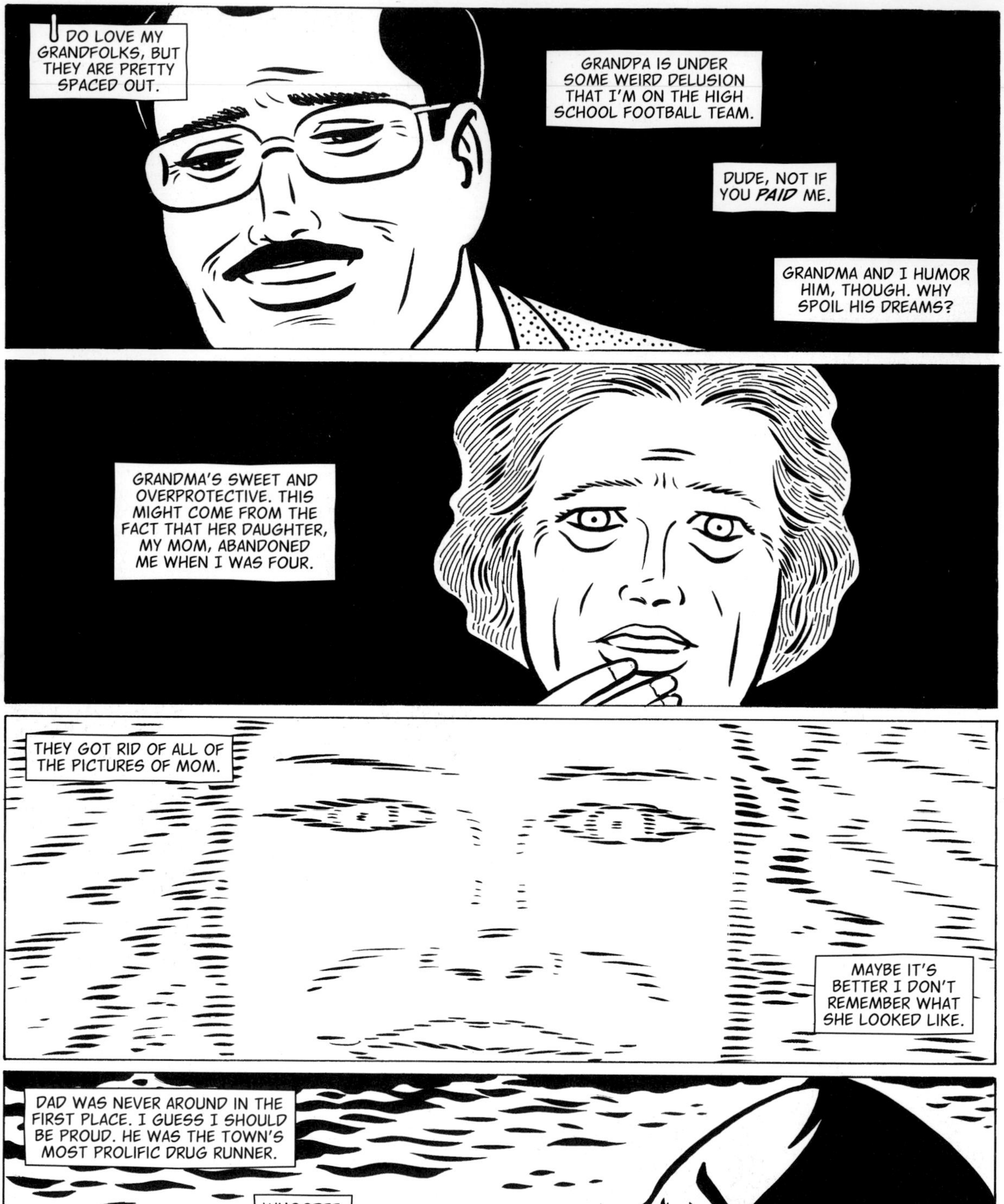
I DO LOVE MY GRANDFOLKS, BUT THEY ARE PRETTY SPACED OUT.
GRANDPA IS UNDER SOME WEIRD DELUSION THAT I'M ON THE HIGH SCHOOL FOOTBALL TEAM.
DUDE, NOT IF YOU *PAID* ME.
GRANDMA AND I HUMOR HIM, THOUGH. WHY SPOIL HIS DREAMS?
GRANDMA'S SWEET AND OVERPROTECTIVE. THIS MIGHT COME FROM THE FACT THAT HER DAUGHTER, MY MOM, ABANDONED ME WHEN I WAS FOUR.
THEY GOT RID OF ALL OF THE PICTURES OF MOM.
MAYBE IT'S BETTER I DON'T REMEMBER WHAT SHE LOOKED LIKE.
DAD WAS NEVER AROUND IN THE FIRST PLACE. I GUESS I SHOULD BE PROUD. HE WAS THE TOWN'S MOST PROLIFIC DRUG RUNNER.
WHOOPEE.
I DO WONDER SOMETIMES WHAT HAPPENED THAT MY GRANDPARENTS RAISED A DAUGHTER WHO'D ABANDON HER SON.

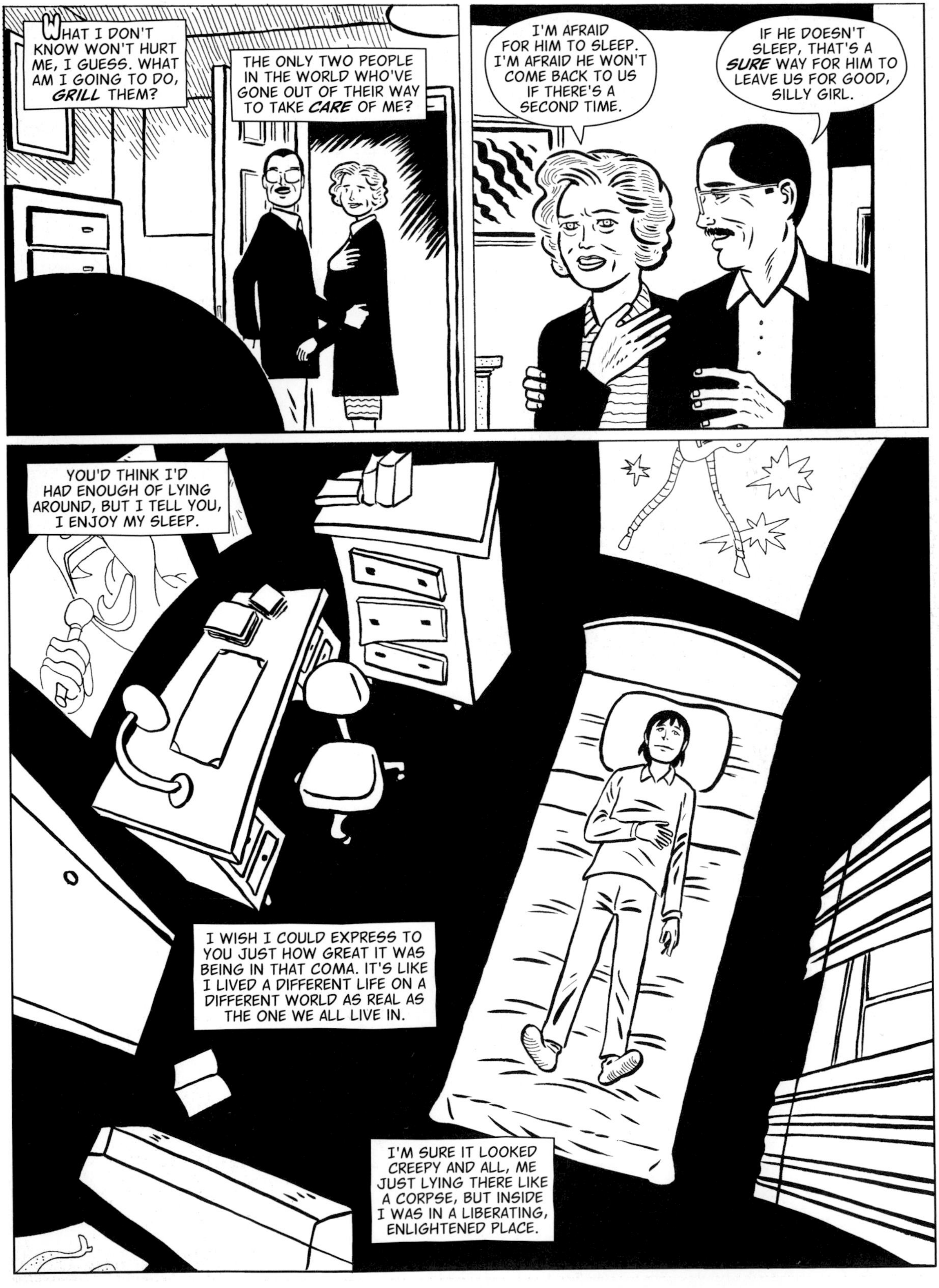
WHAT I DON'T KNOW WON'T HURT ME, I GUESS. WHAT AM I GOING TO DO, GRILL THEM?
THE ONLY TWO PEOPLE IN THE WORLD WHO'VE GONE OUT OF THEIR WAY TO TAKE CARE OF ME?
I'M AFRAID FOR HIM TO SLEEP. I'M AFRAID HE WON'T COME BACK TO US IF THERE'S A SECOND TIME.
IF HE DOESN'T SLEEP, THAT'S A SURE WAY FOR HIM TO LEAVE US FOR GOOD, SILLY GIRL.
YOU'D THINK I'D HAD ENOUGH OF LYING AROUND, BUT I TELL YOU, I ENJOY MY SLEEP.
I WISH I COULD EXPRESS TO YOU JUST HOW GREAT IT WAS BEING IN THAT COMA. IT'S LIKE I LIVED A DIFFERENT LIFE ON A DIFFERENT WORLD AS REAL AS THE ONE WE ALL LIVE IN.
I'M SURE IT LOOKED CREEPY AND ALL, ME JUST LYING THERE LIKE A CORPSE, BUT INSIDE I WAS IN A LIBERATING, ENLIGHTENED PLACE.

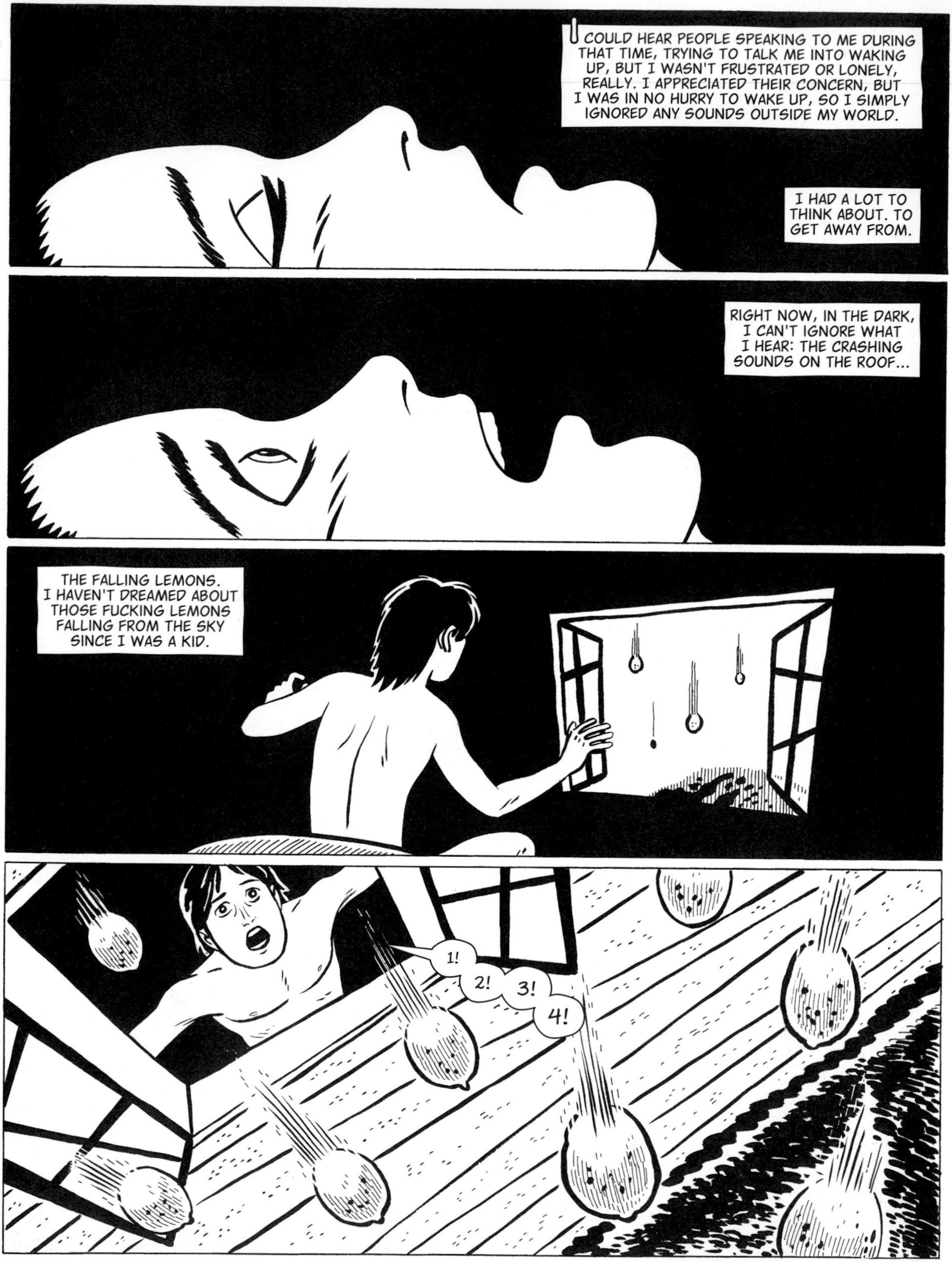
I COULD HEAR PEOPLE SPEAKING TO ME DURING THAT TIME, TRYING TO TALK ME INTO WAKING UP, BUT I WASN'T FRUSTRATED OR LONELY, REALLY. I APPRECIATED THEIR CONCERN, BUT I WAS IN NO HURRY TO WAKE UP, SO I SIMPLY IGNORED ANY SOUNDS OUTSIDE MY WORLD.
I HAD A LOT TO THINK ABOUT. TO GET AWAY FROM.
RIGHT NOW, IN THE DARK, I CAN'T IGNORE WHAT I HEAR: THE CRASHING SOUNDS ON THE ROOF...
THE FALLING LEMONS. I HAVEN'T DREAMED ABOUT THOSE FUCKING LEMONS FALLING FROM THE SKY SINCE I WAS A KID.
1!
2!
3!
4!

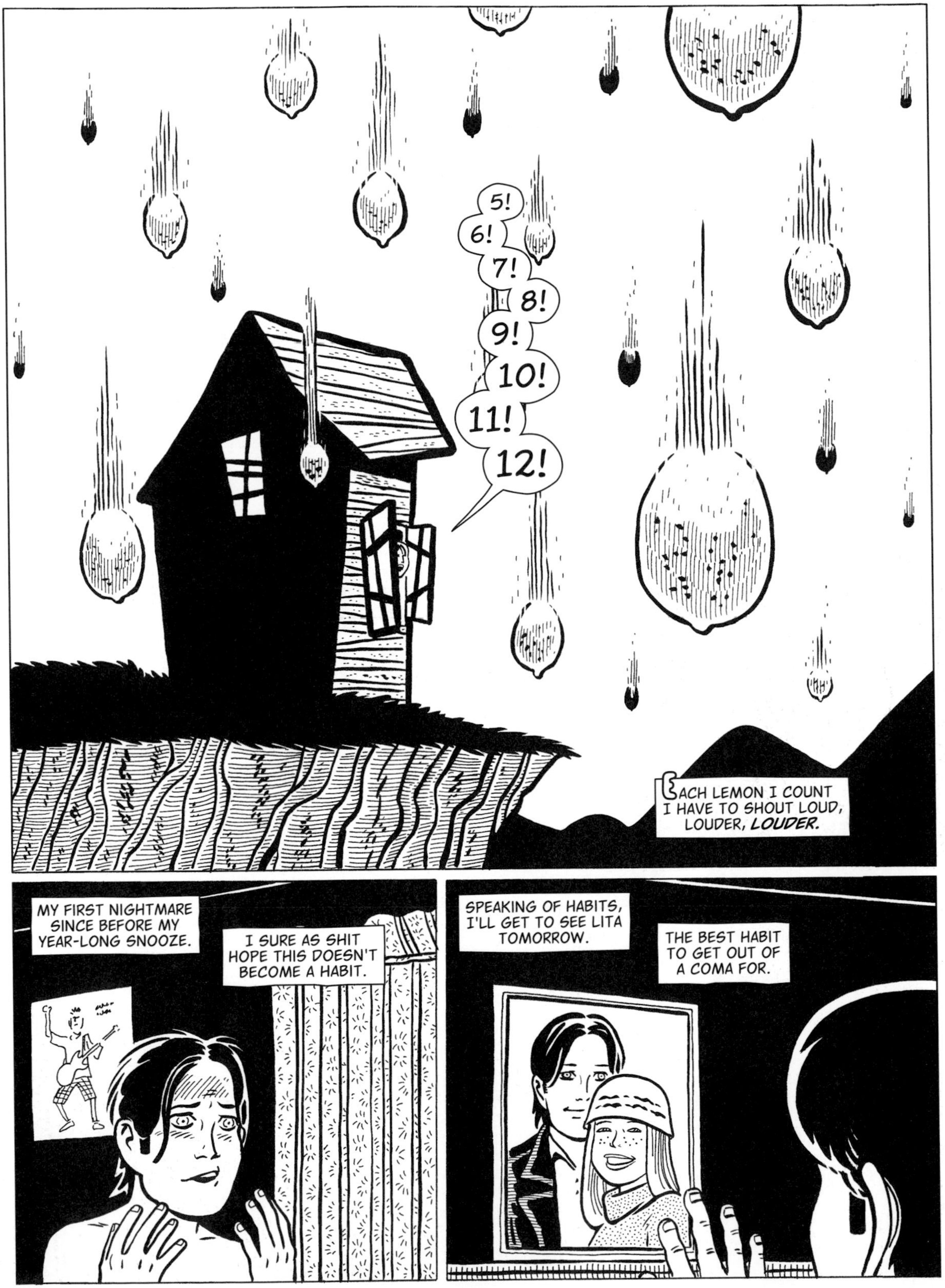
5!
6!
7!
8!
9!
10!
11!
12!
EACH LEMON I COUNT I HAVE TO SHOUT LOUD, LOUDER, *LOUDER.*
MY FIRST NIGHTMARE SINCE BEFORE MY YEAR-LONG SNOOZE.
I SURE AS SHIT HOPE THIS DOESN'T BECOME A HABIT.
SPEAKING OF HABITS, I'LL GET TO SEE LITA TOMORROW.
THE BEST HABIT TO GET OUT OF A COMA FOR.

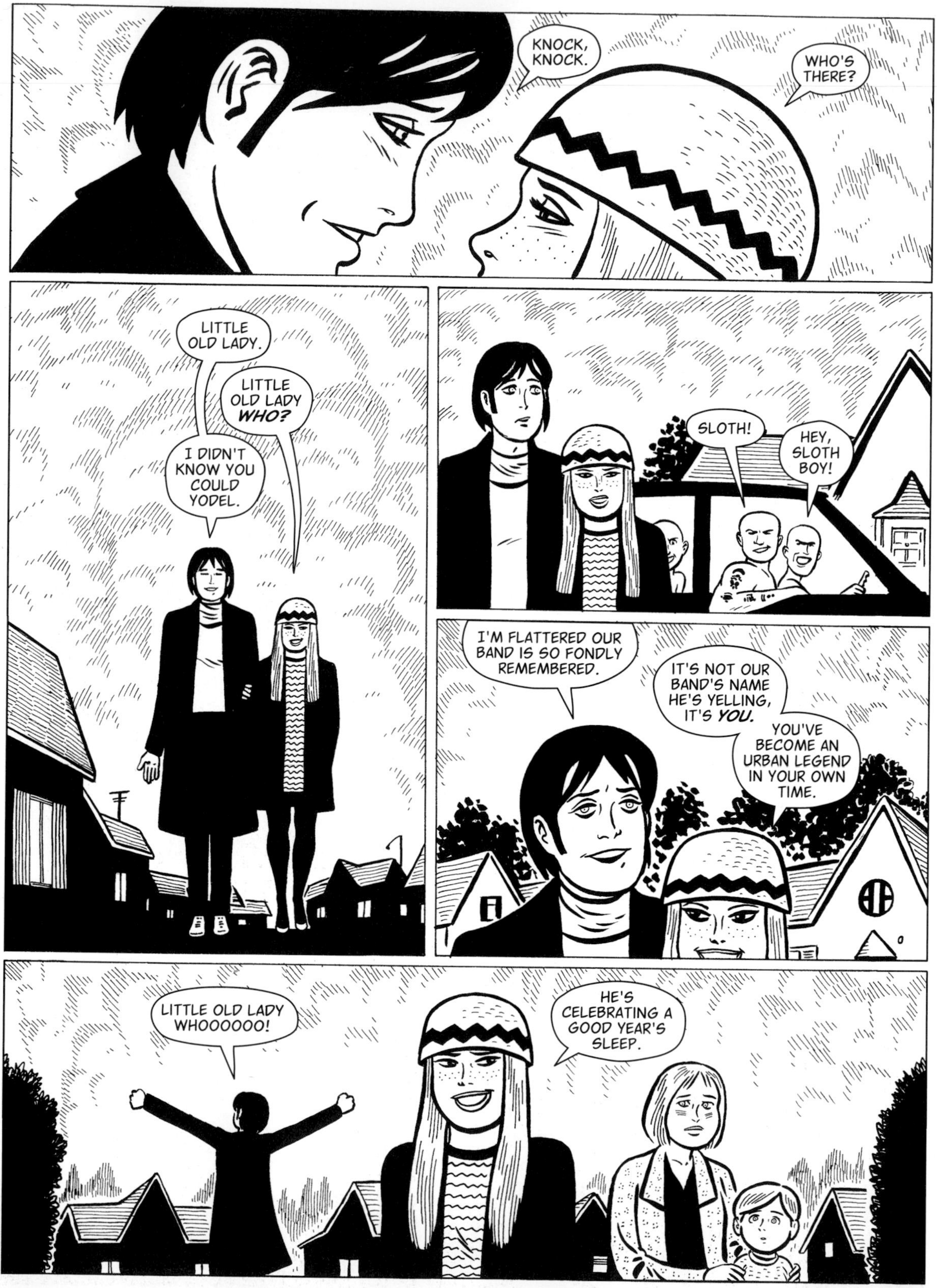
KNOCK, KNOCK.
WHO'S THERE?
LITTLE OLD LADY.
LITTLE OLD LADY *WHO?*
I DIDN'T KNOW YOU COULD YODEL.
SLOTH!
HEY, SLOTH BOY!
I'M FLATTERED OUR BAND IS SO FONDLY REMEMBERED.
IT'S NOT OUR BAND'S NAME HE'S YELLING, IT'S *YOU.*
YOU'VE BECOME AN URBAN LEGEND IN YOUR OWN TIME.
LITTLE OLD LADY WHOOOOOO!
HE'S CELEBRATING A GOOD YEAR'S SLEEP.

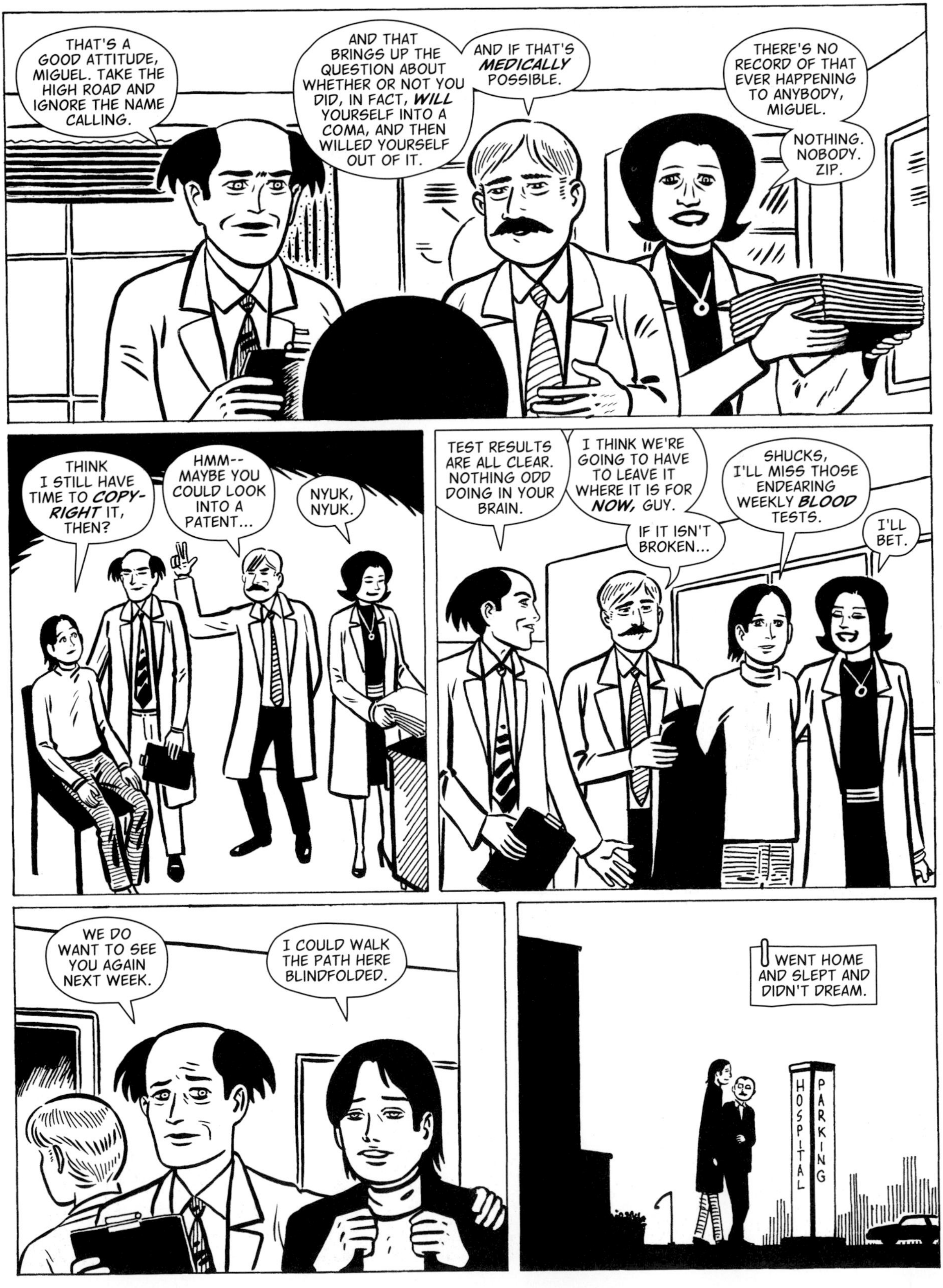

THAT'S A GOOD ATTITUDE, MIGUEL. TAKE THE HIGH ROAD AND IGNORE THE NAME CALLING.
AND THAT BRINGS UP THE QUESTION ABOUT WHETHER OR NOT YOU DID, IN FACT, WILL YOURSELF INTO A COMA, AND THEN WILLED YOURSELF OUT OF IT.
AND IF THAT'S MEDICALLY POSSIBLE.
THERE'S NO RECORD OF THAT EVER HAPPENING TO ANYBODY, MIGUEL.
NOTHING. NOBODY. ZIP.
THINK I STILL HAVE TIME TO COPY-RIGHT IT, THEN?
HMM-- MAYBE YOU COULD LOOK INTO A PATENT...
NYUK, NYUK.
TEST RESULTS ARE ALL CLEAR. NOTHING ODD DOING IN YOUR BRAIN.
I THINK WE'RE GOING TO HAVE TO LEAVE IT WHERE IT IS FOR NOW, GUY.
IF IT ISN'T BROKEN...
SHUCKS, I'LL MISS THOSE ENDEARING WEEKLY BLOOD TESTS.
I'LL BET.
WE DO WANT TO SEE YOU AGAIN NEXT WEEK.
I COULD WALK THE PATH HERE BLINDFOLDED.
I WENT HOME AND SLEPT AND DIDN'T DREAM.
HOSPITAL PARKING

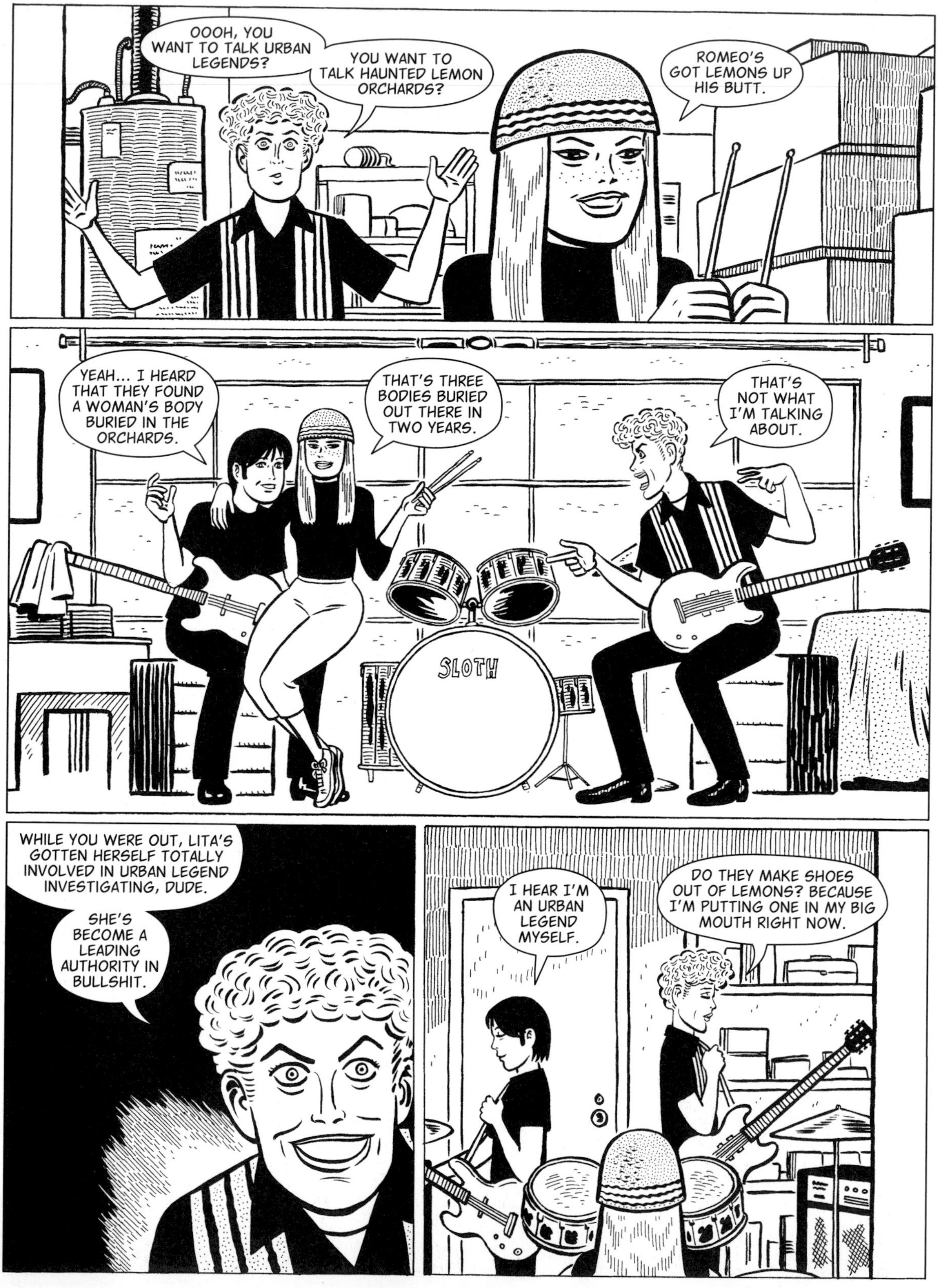
OOOH, YOU WANT TO TALK URBAN LEGENDS?
YOU WANT TO TALK HAUNTED LEMON ORCHARDS?
ROMEO'S GOT LEMONS UP HIS BUTT.
YEAH... I HEARD THAT THEY FOUND A WOMAN'S BODY BURIED IN THE ORCHARDS.
THAT'S THREE BODIES BURIED OUT THERE IN TWO YEARS.
THAT'S NOT WHAT I'M TALKING ABOUT.
SLOTH
WHILE YOU WERE OUT, LITA'S GOTTEN HERSELF TOTALLY INVOLVED IN URBAN LEGEND INVESTIGATING, DUDE.
SHE'S BECOME A LEADING AUTHORITY IN BULLSHIT.
I HEAR I'M AN URBAN LEGEND MYSELF.
DO THEY MAKE SHOES OUT OF LEMONS? BECAUSE I'M PUTTING ONE IN MY BIG MOUTH RIGHT NOW.

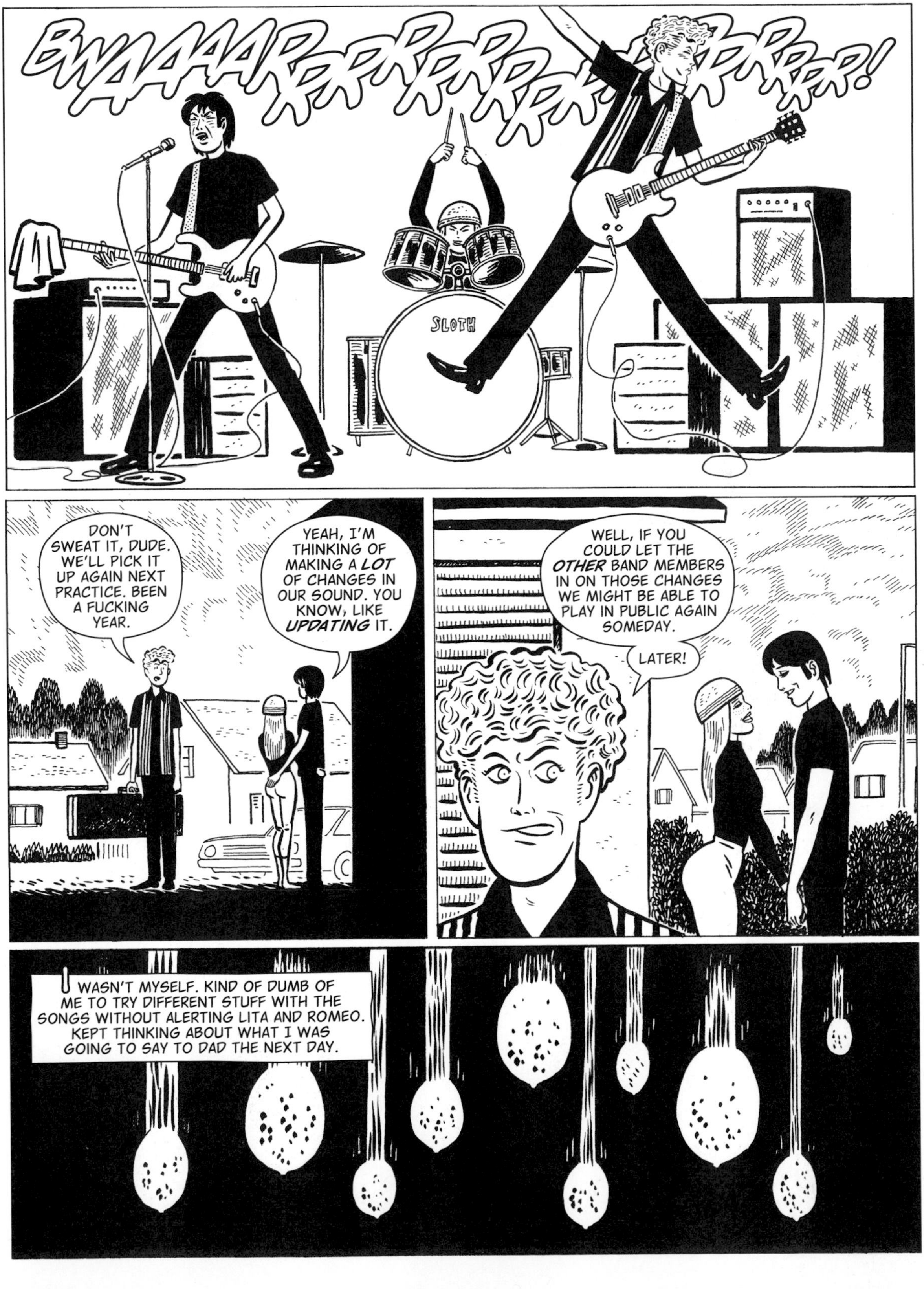
BWAAAAARRRRRRRRRRRRRRRRRRRR!
SLOTH
DON'T SWEAT IT, DUDE. WE'LL PICK IT UP AGAIN NEXT PRACTICE. BEEN A FUCKING YEAR.
YEAH, I'M THINKING OF MAKING A *LOT* OF CHANGES IN OUR SOUND. YOU KNOW, LIKE *UPDATING* IT.
WELL, IF YOU COULD LET THE *OTHER* BAND MEMBERS IN ON THOSE CHANGES WE MIGHT BE ABLE TO PLAY IN PUBLIC AGAIN SOMEDAY.
LATER!
I WASN'T MYSELF. KIND OF DUMB OF ME TO TRY DIFFERENT STUFF WITH THE SONGS WITHOUT ALERTING LITA AND ROMEO. KEPT THINKING ABOUT WHAT I WAS GOING TO SAY TO DAD THE NEXT DAY.

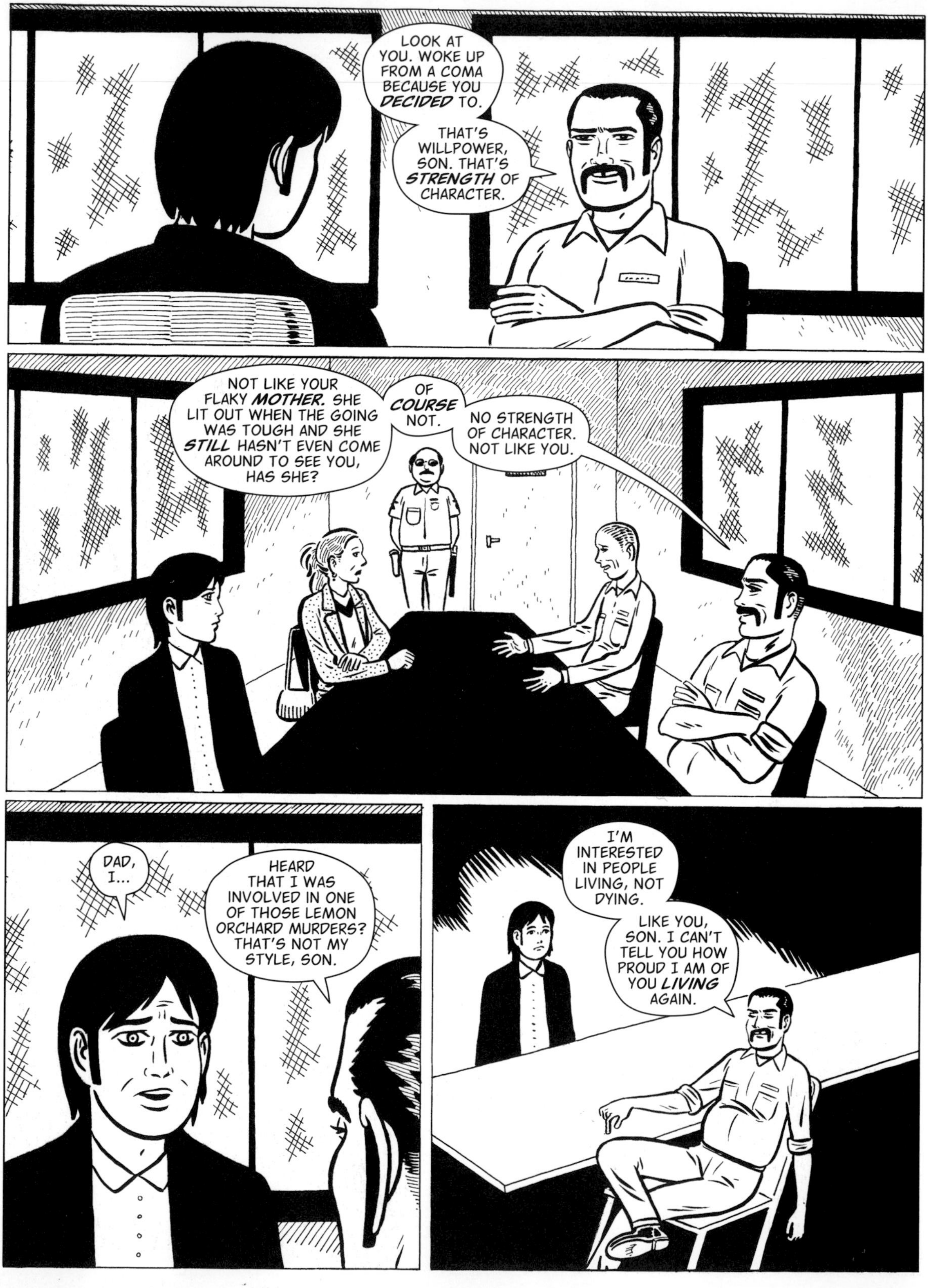
LOOK AT YOU. WOKE UP FROM A COMA BECAUSE YOU DECIDED TO.
THAT'S WILLPOWER, SON. THAT'S STRENGTH OF CHARACTER.
NOT LIKE YOUR FLAKY MOTHER. SHE LIT OUT WHEN THE GOING WAS TOUGH AND SHE STILL HASN'T EVEN COME AROUND TO SEE YOU, HAS SHE?
OF COURSE NOT.
NO STRENGTH OF CHARACTER. NOT LIKE YOU.
DAD, I...
HEARD THAT I WAS INVOLVED IN ONE OF THOSE LEMON ORCHARD MURDERS? THAT'S NOT MY STYLE, SON.
I'M INTERESTED IN PEOPLE LIVING, NOT DYING.
LIKE YOU, SON. I CAN'T TELL YOU HOW PROUD I AM OF YOU LIVING AGAIN.

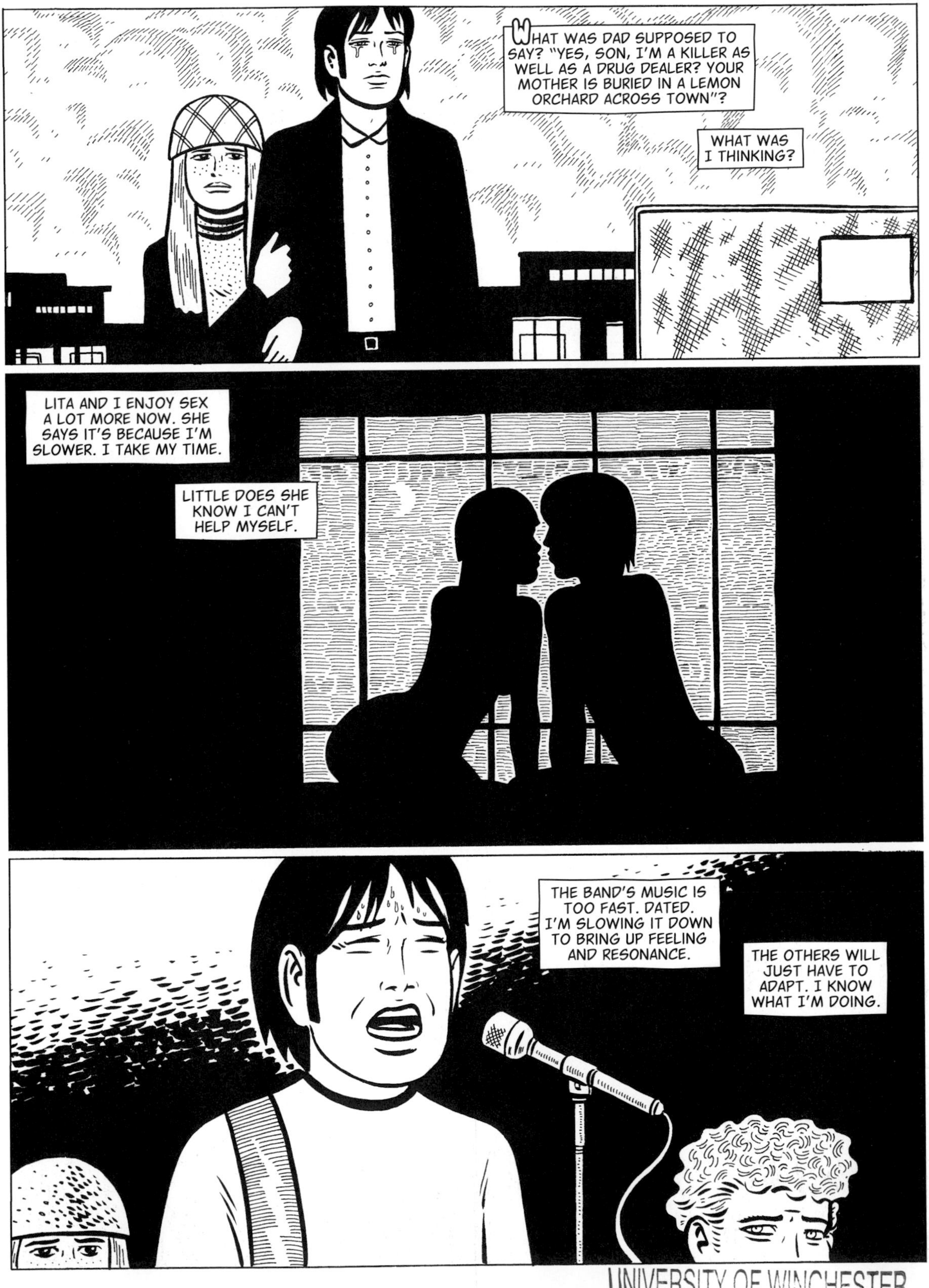
WHAT WAS DAD SUPPOSED TO SAY? "YES, SON, I'M A KILLER AS WELL AS A DRUG DEALER? YOUR MOTHER IS BURIED IN A LEMON ORCHARD ACROSS TOWN"?
WHAT WAS I THINKING?
LITA AND I ENJOY SEX A LOT MORE NOW. SHE SAYS IT'S BECAUSE I'M SLOWER. I TAKE MY TIME.
LITTLE DOES SHE KNOW I CAN'T HELP MYSELF.
THE BAND'S MUSIC IS TOO FAST. DATED. I'M SLOWING IT DOWN TO BRING UP FEELING AND RESONANCE.
THE OTHERS WILL JUST HAVE TO ADAPT. I KNOW WHAT I'M DOING.

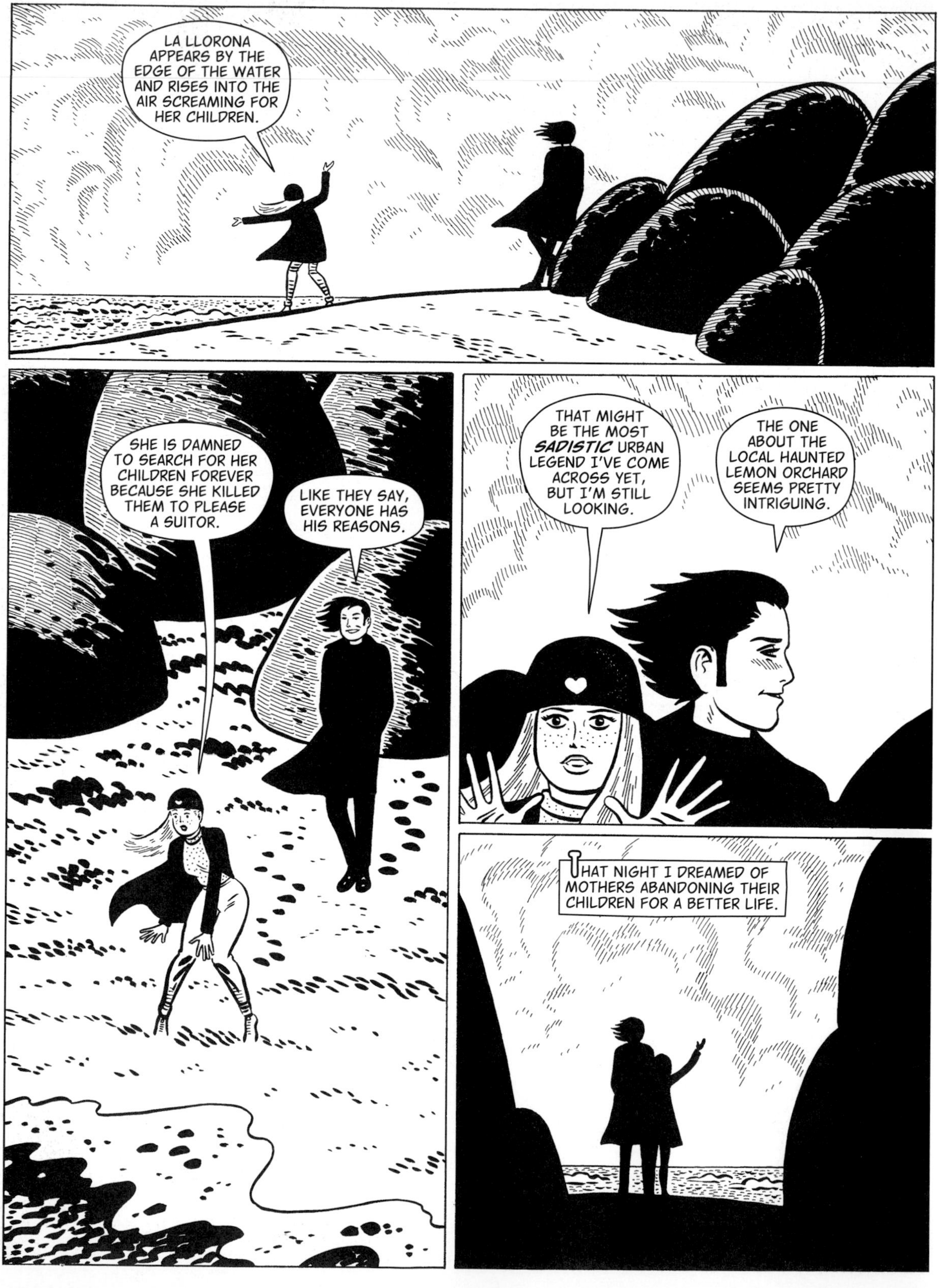
LA LLORONA APPEARS BY THE EDGE OF THE WATER AND RISES INTO THE AIR SCREAMING FOR HER CHILDREN.
SHE IS DAMNED TO SEARCH FOR HER CHILDREN FOREVER BECAUSE SHE KILLED THEM TO PLEASE A SUITOR.
LIKE THEY SAY, EVERYONE HAS HIS REASONS.
THAT MIGHT BE THE MOST SADISTIC URBAN LEGEND I'VE COME ACROSS YET, BUT I'M STILL LOOKING.
THE ONE ABOUT THE LOCAL HAUNTED LEMON ORCHARD SEEMS PRETTY INTRIGUING.
THAT NIGHT I DREAMED OF MOTHERS ABANDONING THEIR CHILDREN FOR A BETTER LIFE.

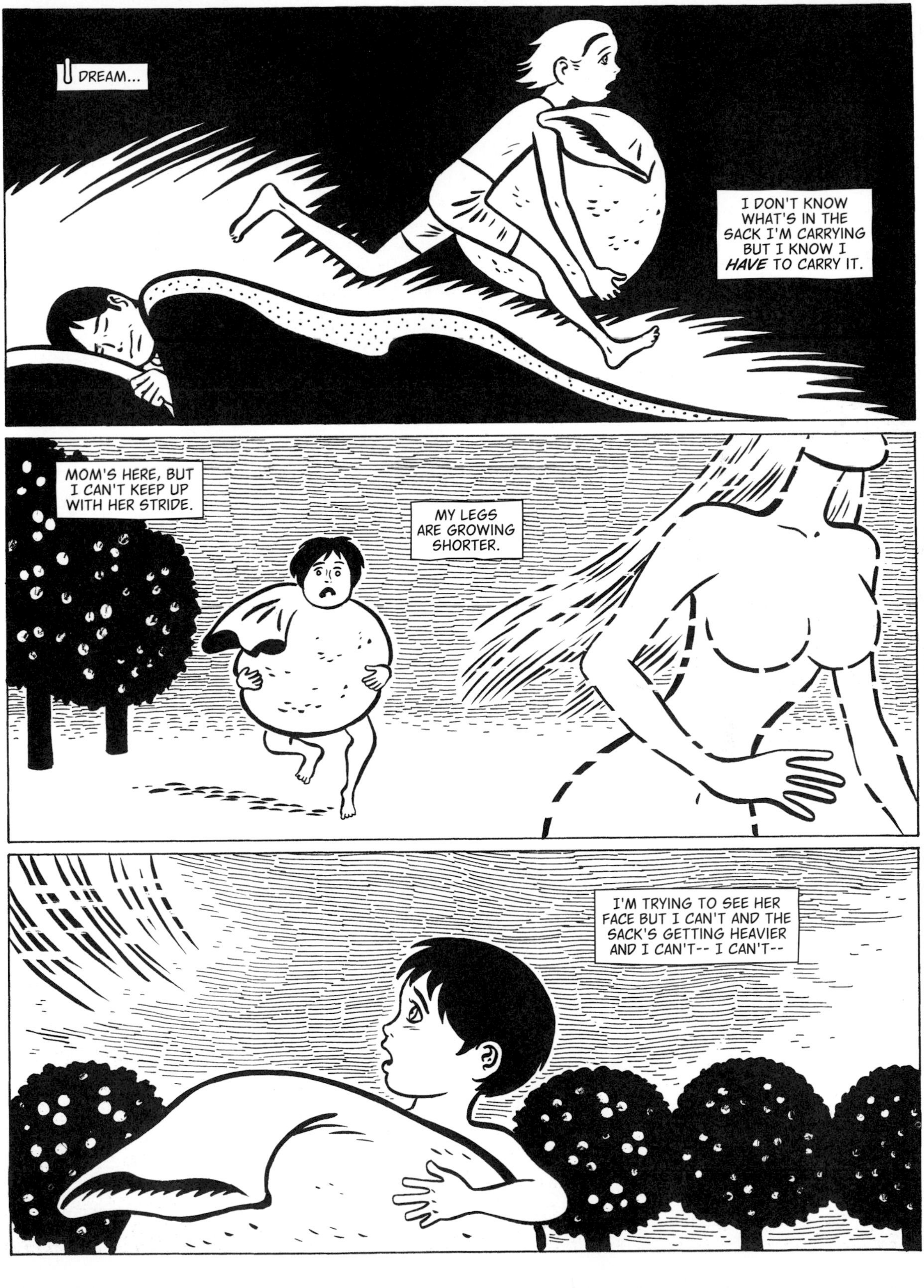
I DREAM...
I DON'T KNOW WHAT'S IN THE SACK I'M CARRYING BUT I KNOW I *HAVE* TO CARRY IT.
MOM'S HERE, BUT I CAN'T KEEP UP WITH HER STRIDE.
MY LEGS ARE GROWING SHORTER.
I'M TRYING TO SEE HER FACE BUT I CAN'T AND THE SACK'S GETTING HEAVIER AND I CAN'T-- I CAN'T--

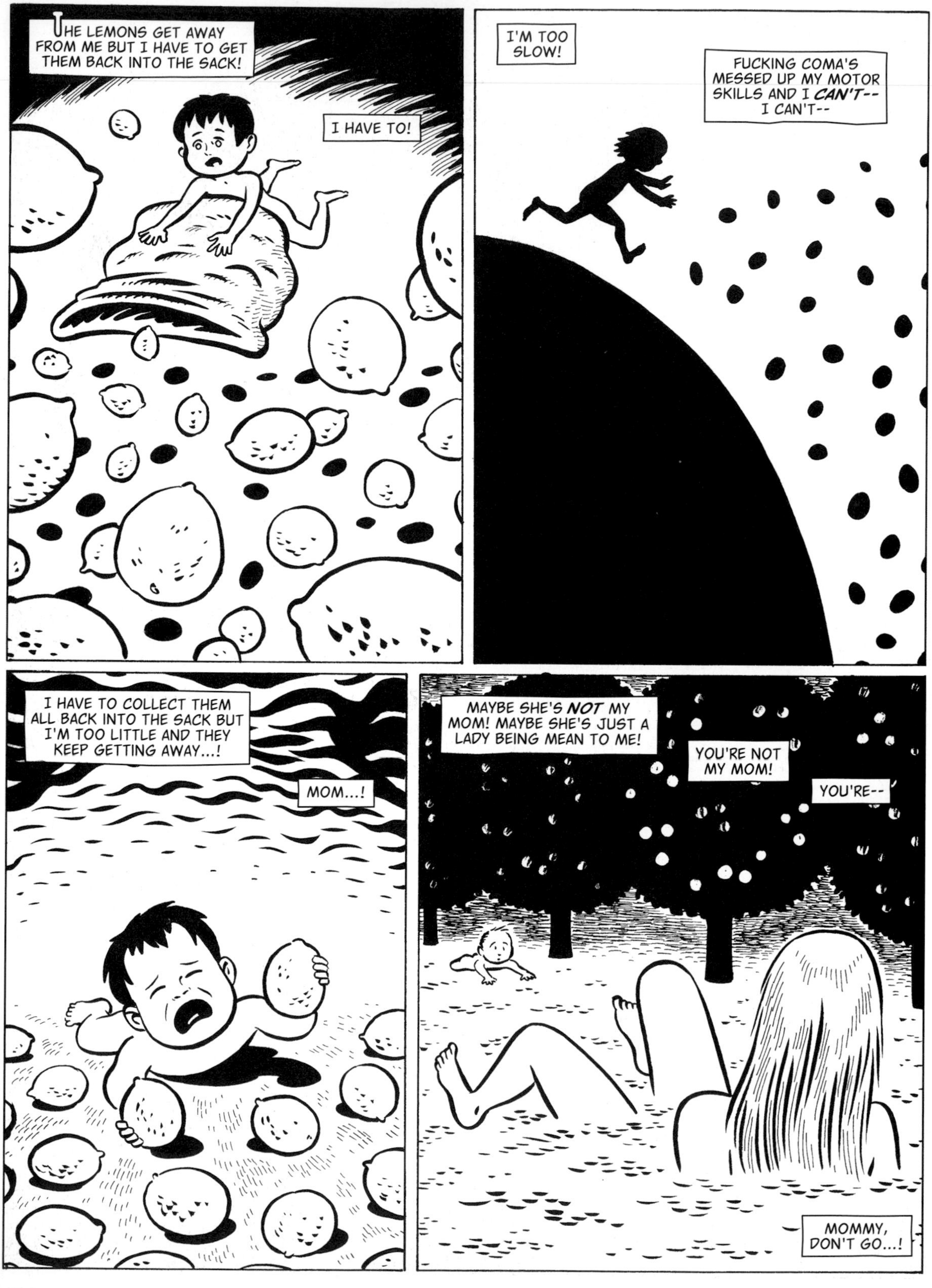
THE LEMONS GET AWAY FROM ME BUT I HAVE TO GET THEM BACK INTO THE SACK!
I HAVE TO!
I'M TOO SLOW!
FUCKING COMA'S MESSED UP MY MOTOR SKILLS AND I CAN'T-- I CAN'T--
I HAVE TO COLLECT THEM ALL BACK INTO THE SACK BUT I'M TOO LITTLE AND THEY KEEP GETTING AWAY...!
MOM...!
MAYBE SHE'S NOT MY MOM! MAYBE SHE'S JUST A LADY BEING MEAN TO ME!
YOU'RE NOT MY MOM!
YOU'RE--
MOMMY, DON'T GO...!

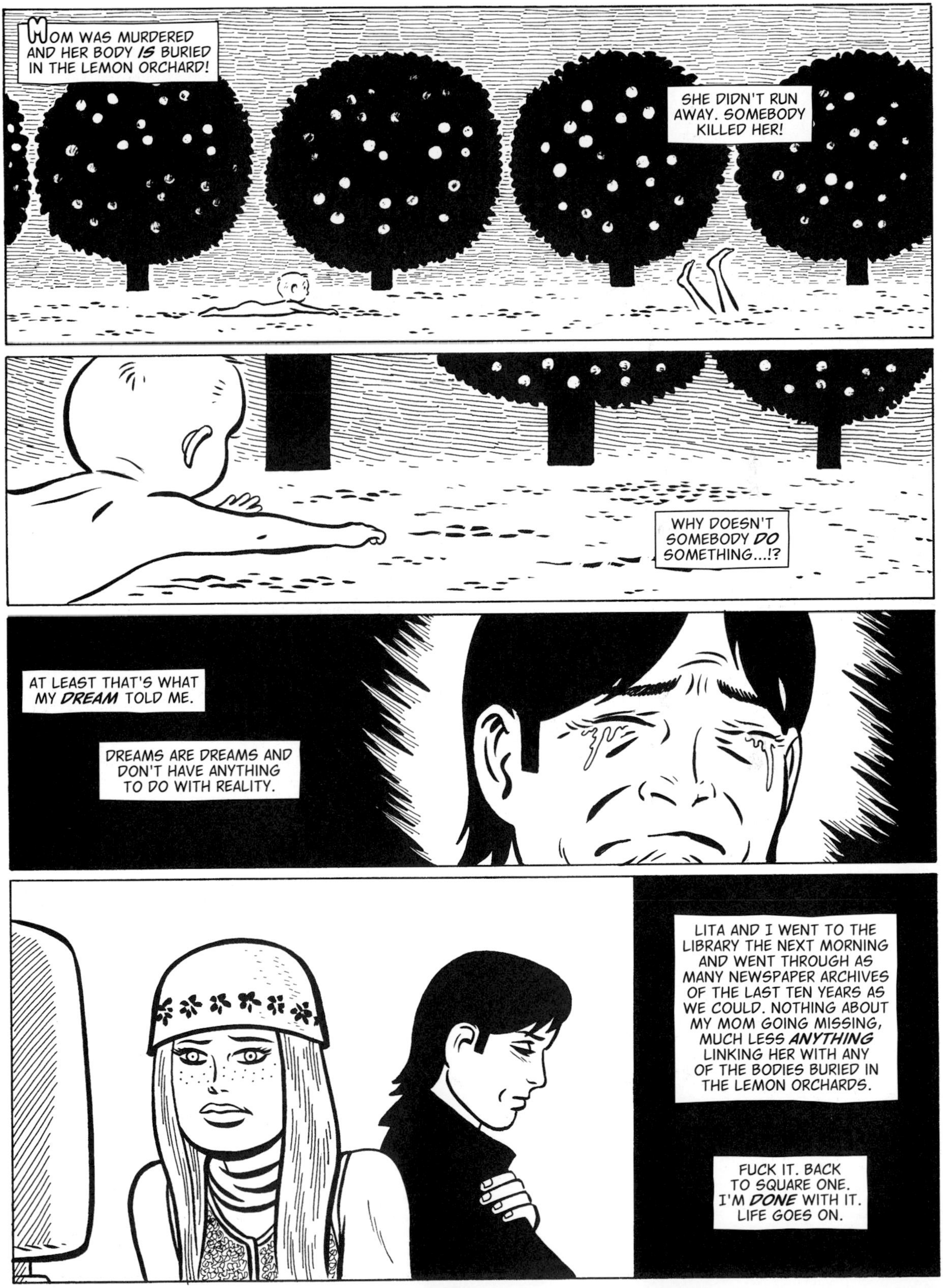
MOM WAS MURDERED AND HER BODY IS BURIED IN THE LEMON ORCHARD!
SHE DIDN'T RUN AWAY. SOMEBODY KILLED HER!
WHY DOESN'T SOMEBODY DO SOMETHING...!?
AT LEAST THAT'S WHAT MY DREAM TOLD ME.
DREAMS ARE DREAMS AND DON'T HAVE ANYTHING TO DO WITH REALITY.
LITA AND I WENT TO THE LIBRARY THE NEXT MORNING AND WENT THROUGH AS MANY NEWSPAPER ARCHIVES OF THE LAST TEN YEARS AS WE COULD. NOTHING ABOUT MY MOM GOING MISSING, MUCH LESS ANYTHING LINKING HER WITH ANY OF THE BODIES BURIED IN THE LEMON ORCHARDS.
FUCK IT. BACK TO SQUARE ONE. I'M DONE WITH IT. LIFE GOES ON.

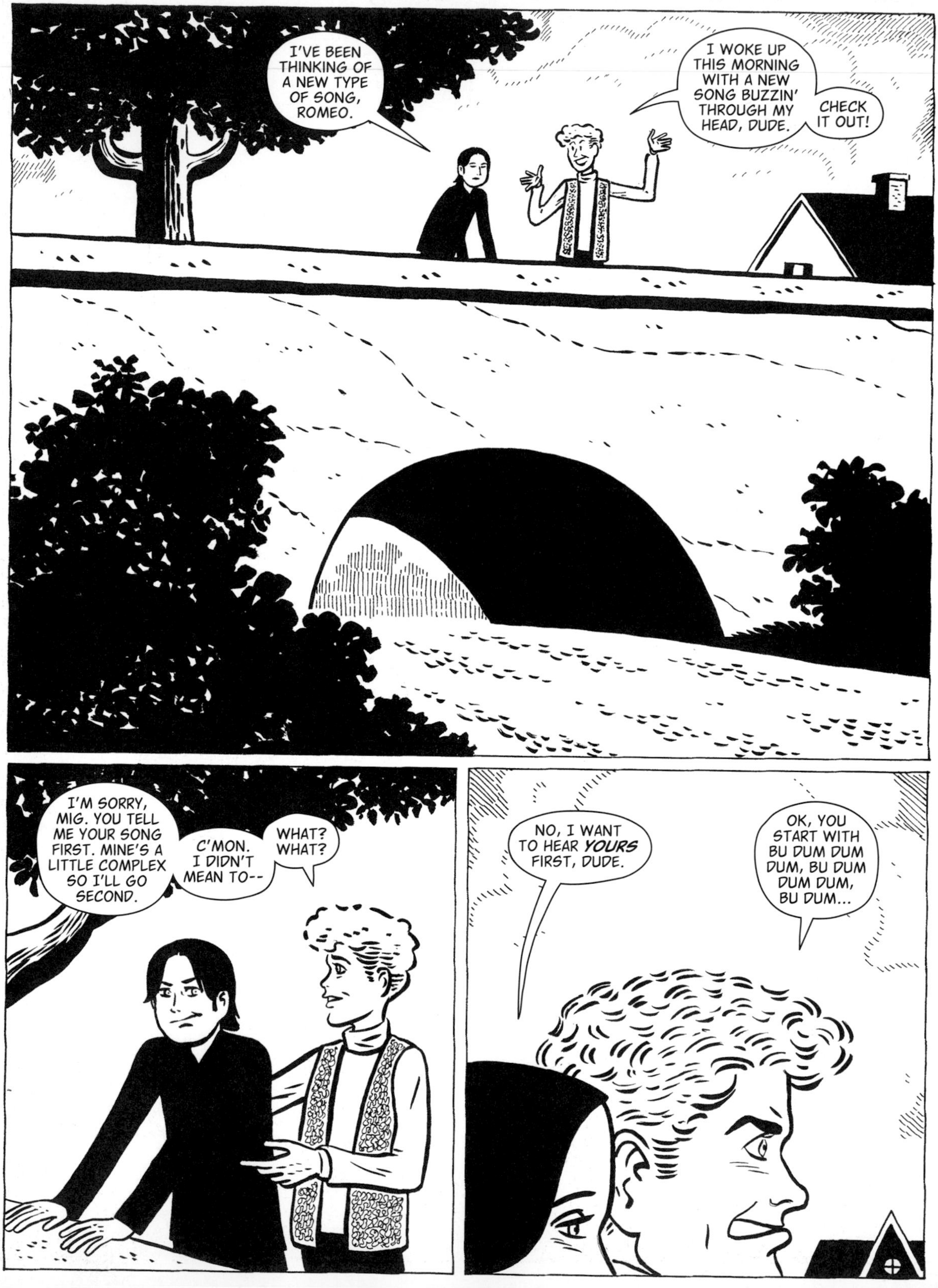
I'VE BEEN THINKING OF A NEW TYPE OF SONG, ROMEO.
I WOKE UP THIS MORNING WITH A NEW SONG BUZZIN' THROUGH MY HEAD, DUDE.
CHECK IT OUT!
I'M SORRY, MIG. YOU TELL ME YOUR SONG FIRST. MINE'S A LITTLE COMPLEX SO I'LL GO SECOND.
C'MON. I DIDN'T MEAN TO--
WHAT? WHAT?
NO, I WANT TO HEAR ***YOURS*** FIRST, DUDE.
OK, YOU START WITH BU DUM DUM DUM, BU DUM DUM DUM, BU DUM...

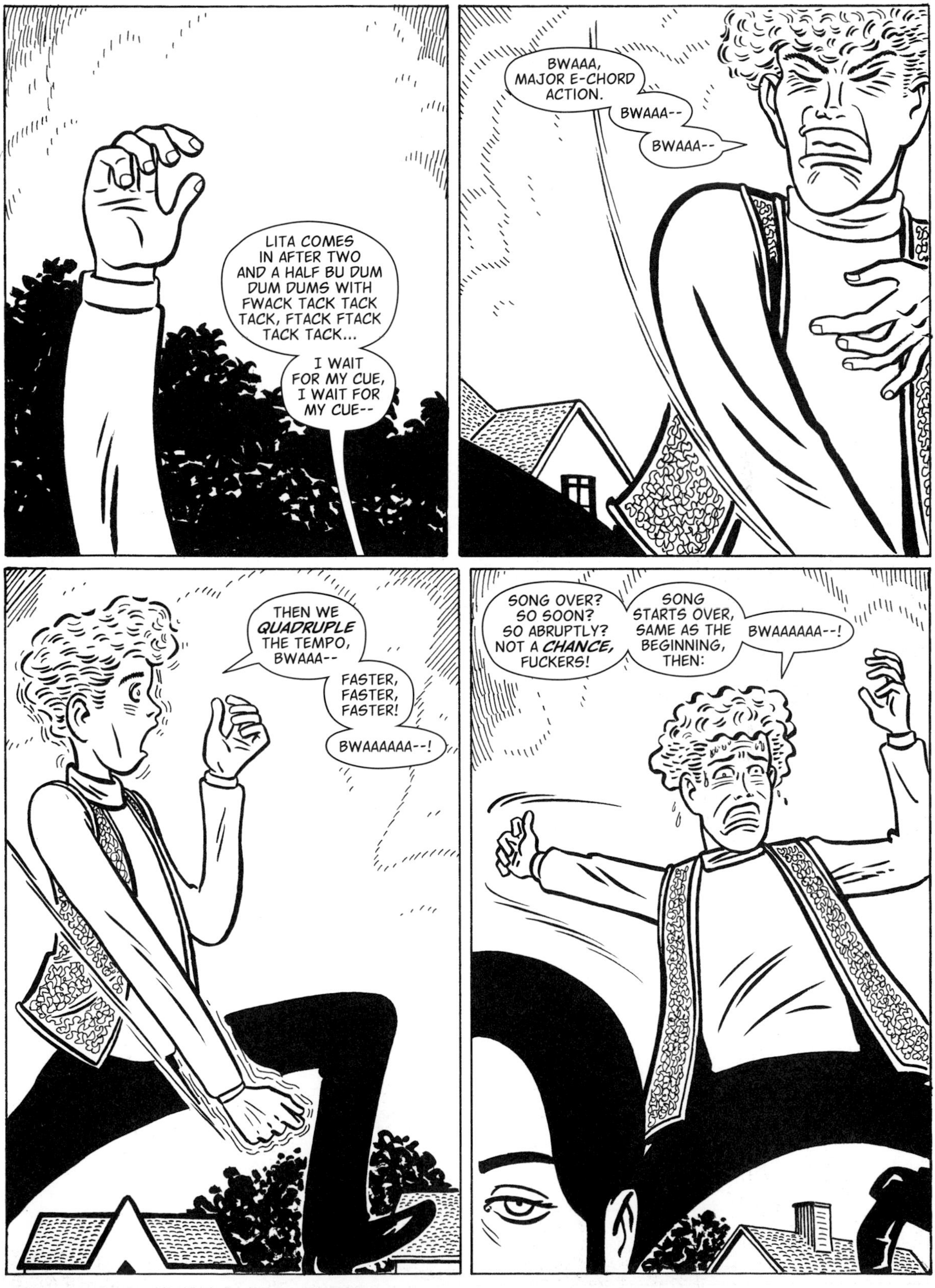
LITA COMES IN AFTER TWO AND A HALF BU DUM DUM DUMS WITH FWACK TACK TACK TACK, FTACK FTACK TACK TACK...
I WAIT FOR MY CUE, I WAIT FOR MY CUE--
BWAAA, MAJOR E-CHORD ACTION.
BWAAA--
BWAAA--
THEN WE *QUADRUPLE* THE TEMPO, BWAAA--
FASTER, FASTER, FASTER!
BWAAAAAA--!
SONG OVER? SO SOON? SO ABRUPTLY? NOT A *CHANCE,* FUCKERS!
SONG STARTS OVER, SAME AS THE BEGINNING, THEN:
BWAAAAAA--!

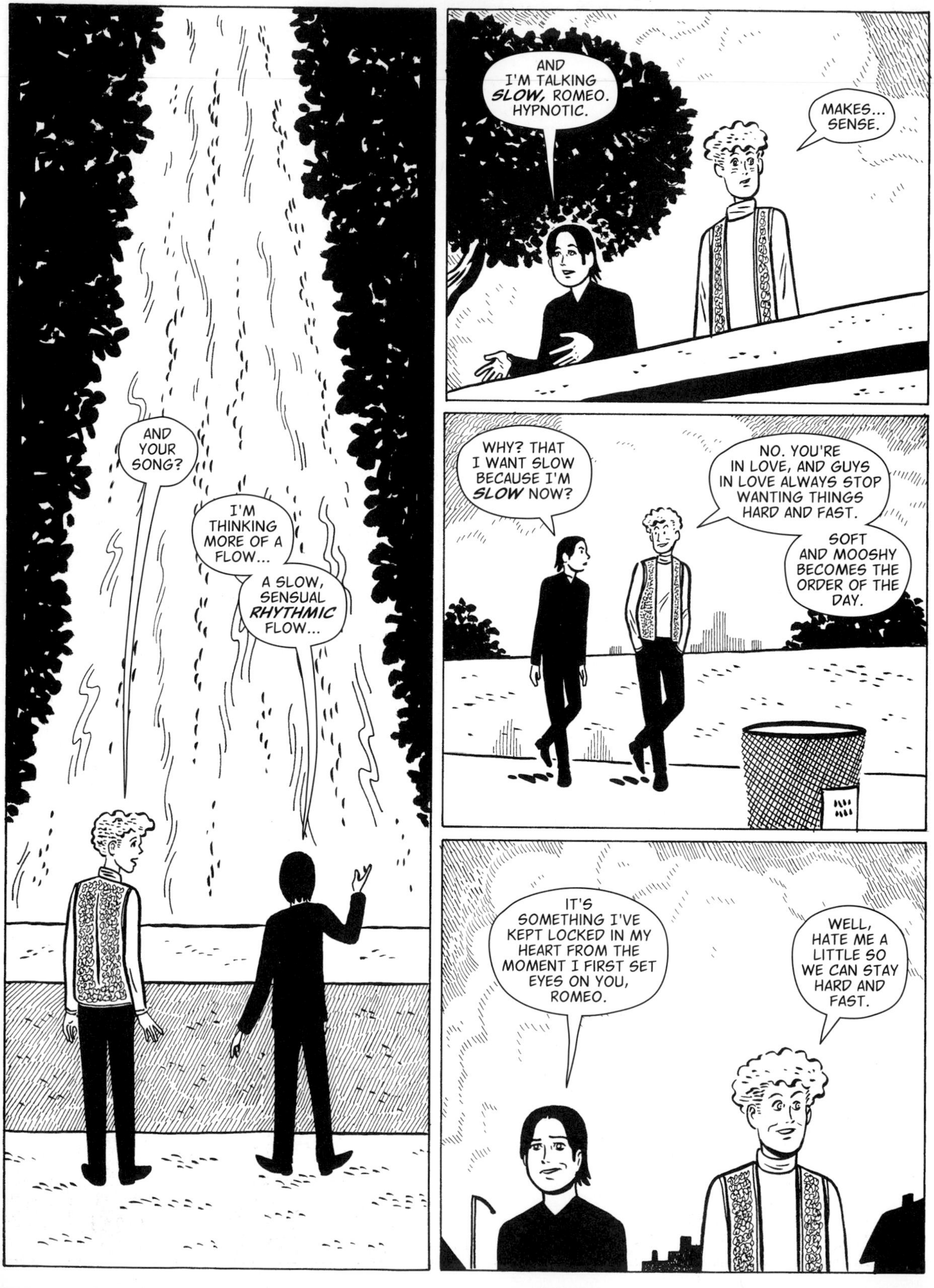
AND YOUR SONG?
I'M THINKING MORE OF A FLOW...
A SLOW, SENSUAL *RHYTHMIC* FLOW...
AND I'M TALKING *SLOW,* ROMEO. HYPNOTIC.
MAKES... SENSE.
WHY? THAT I WANT SLOW BECAUSE I'M *SLOW* NOW?
NO. YOU'RE IN LOVE, AND GUYS IN LOVE ALWAYS STOP WANTING THINGS HARD AND FAST.
SOFT AND MOOSHY BECOMES THE ORDER OF THE DAY.
IT'S SOMETHING I'VE KEPT LOCKED IN MY HEART FROM THE MOMENT I FIRST SET EYES ON YOU, ROMEO.
WELL, HATE ME A LITTLE SO WE CAN STAY HARD AND FAST.

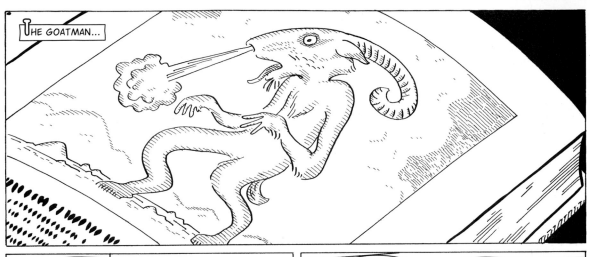

THE GOATMAN...

THE GOATMAN? THE COOLEST OF THE LOCAL LEGENDS BY FAR.

THE GOAT-MAN...

I *REMEMBER* SOMETHING ABOUT THAT, NOW THAT YOU... THE GOATMAN...

HANGS OUT IN THE LEMON ORCHARDS WATCHING OVER THE SPIRITS OF THE DEAD AND BURIED THERE.

THAT'S *ONE* VERSION OF THE LEGEND, ANYWAY.

THERE'S ALL *KINDS* OF VARIATIONS ON THE LEGEND...

YEAH... I REMEMBER SOMETHING ABOUT THAT HE'S TRAPPED THERE...

UNTIL SOMETHING...

OH, YEAH. IF YOU SEE HIM HE'LL TRY TO SWITCH PLACES WITH YOU.

YOU BECOME A GOATMAN AND HE BECOMES *YOU.*

OR YOU. A GOAT-*WOMAN.*

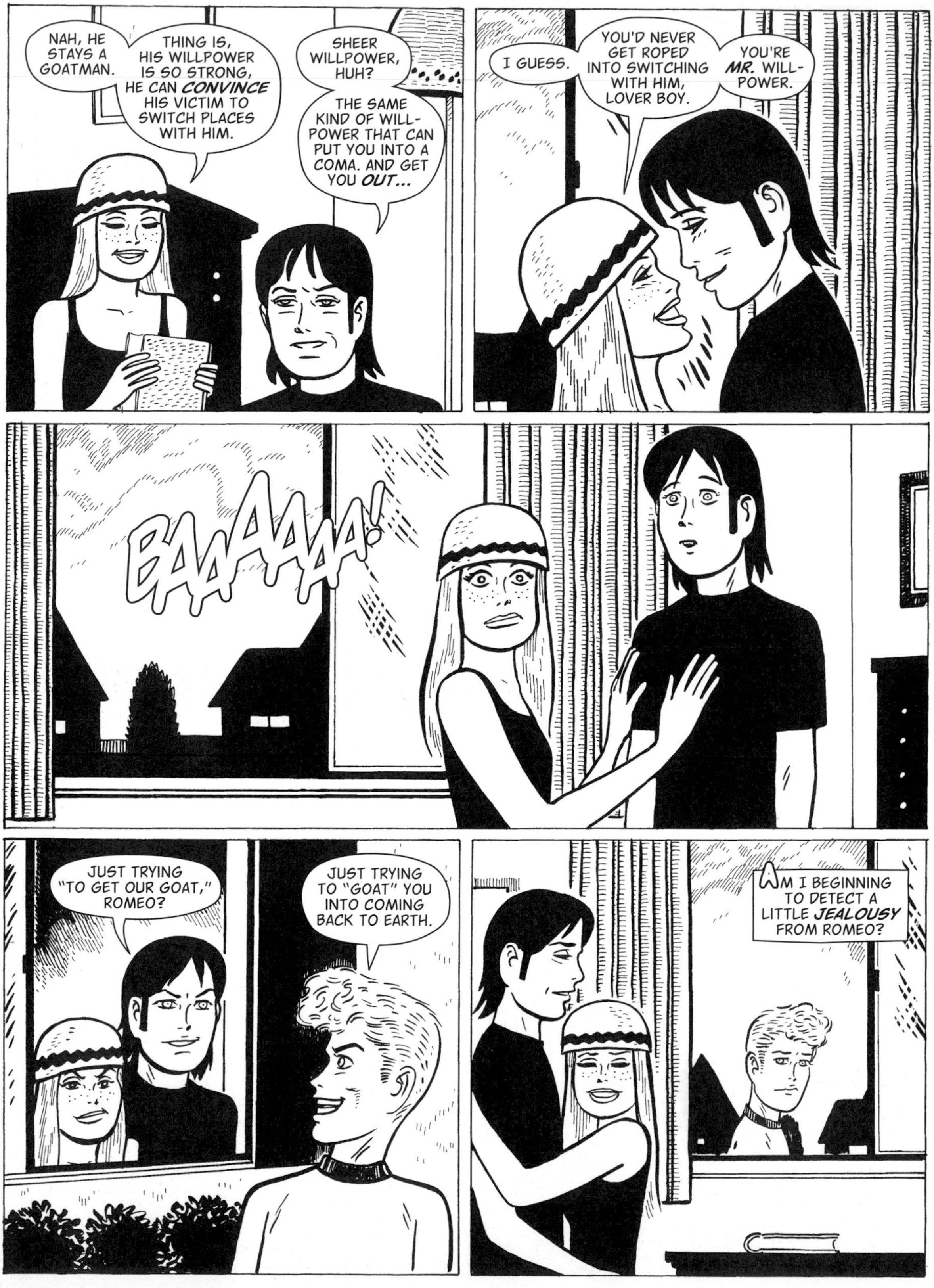
NAH, HE STAYS A GOATMAN.
THING IS, HIS WILLPOWER IS SO STRONG, HE CAN CONVINCE HIS VICTIM TO SWITCH PLACES WITH HIM.
SHEER WILLPOWER, HUH?
THE SAME KIND OF WILL-POWER THAT CAN PUT YOU INTO A COMA. AND GET YOU OUT...
I GUESS.
YOU'D NEVER GET ROPED INTO SWITCHING WITH HIM, LOVER BOY.
YOU'RE MR. WILL-POWER.
BAAAAAA!
JUST TRYING "TO GET OUR GOAT," ROMEO?
JUST TRYING TO "GOAT" YOU INTO COMING BACK TO EARTH.
AM I BEGINNING TO DETECT A LITTLE JEALOUSY FROM ROMEO?

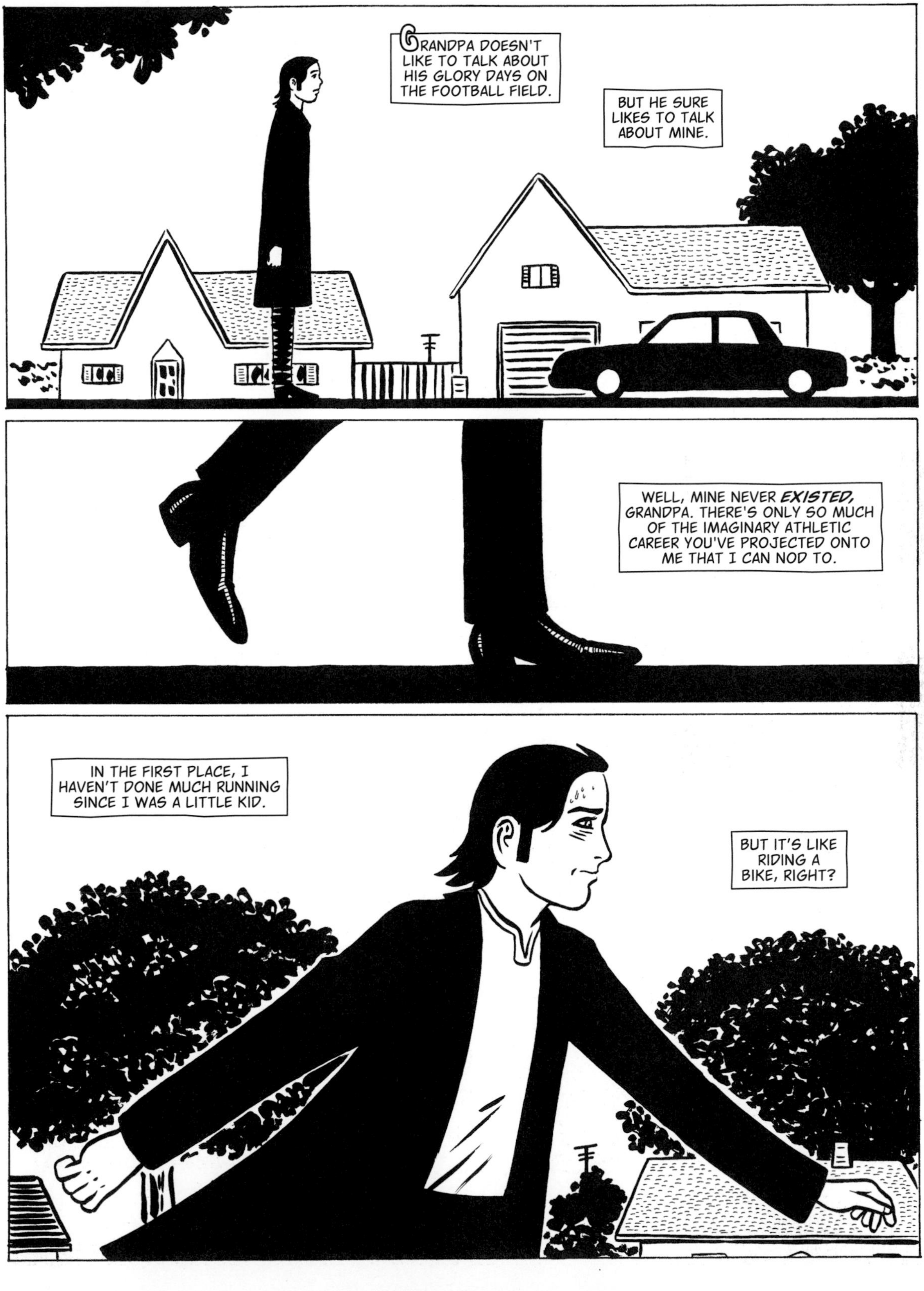
GRANDPA DOESN'T LIKE TO TALK ABOUT HIS GLORY DAYS ON THE FOOTBALL FIELD.
BUT HE SURE LIKES TO TALK ABOUT MINE.
WELL, MINE NEVER *EXISTED,* GRANDPA. THERE'S ONLY SO MUCH OF THE IMAGINARY ATHLETIC CAREER YOU'VE PROJECTED ONTO ME THAT I CAN NOD TO.
IN THE FIRST PLACE, I HAVEN'T DONE MUCH RUNNING SINCE I WAS A LITTLE KID.
BUT IT'S LIKE RIDING A BIKE, RIGHT?

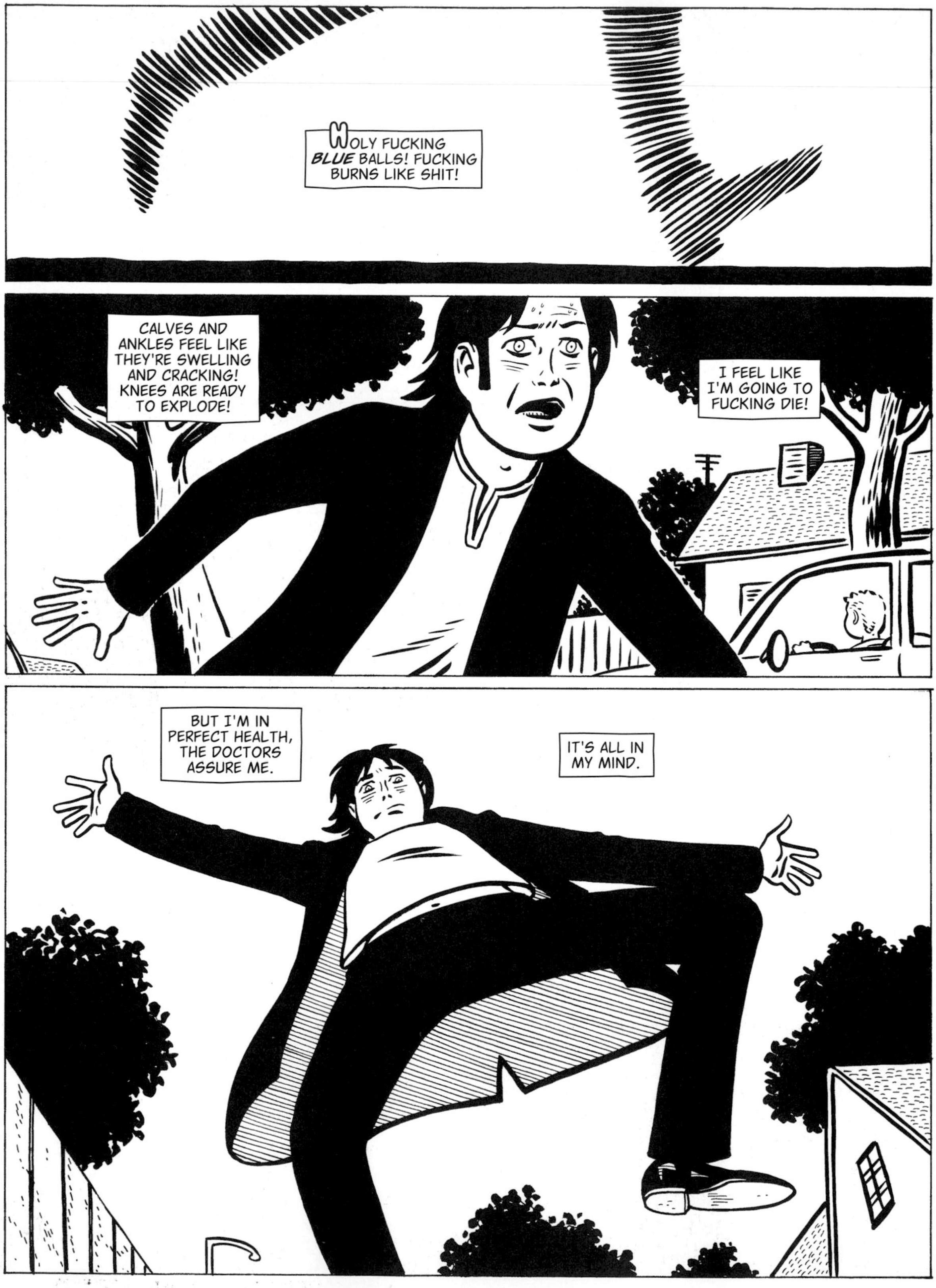
HOLY FUCKING BLUE BALLS! FUCKING BURNS LIKE SHIT!
CALVES AND ANKLES FEEL LIKE THEY'RE SWELLING AND CRACKING! KNEES ARE READY TO EXPLODE!
I FEEL LIKE I'M GOING TO FUCKING DIE!
BUT I'M IN PERFECT HEALTH, THE DOCTORS ASSURE ME.
IT'S ALL IN MY MIND.

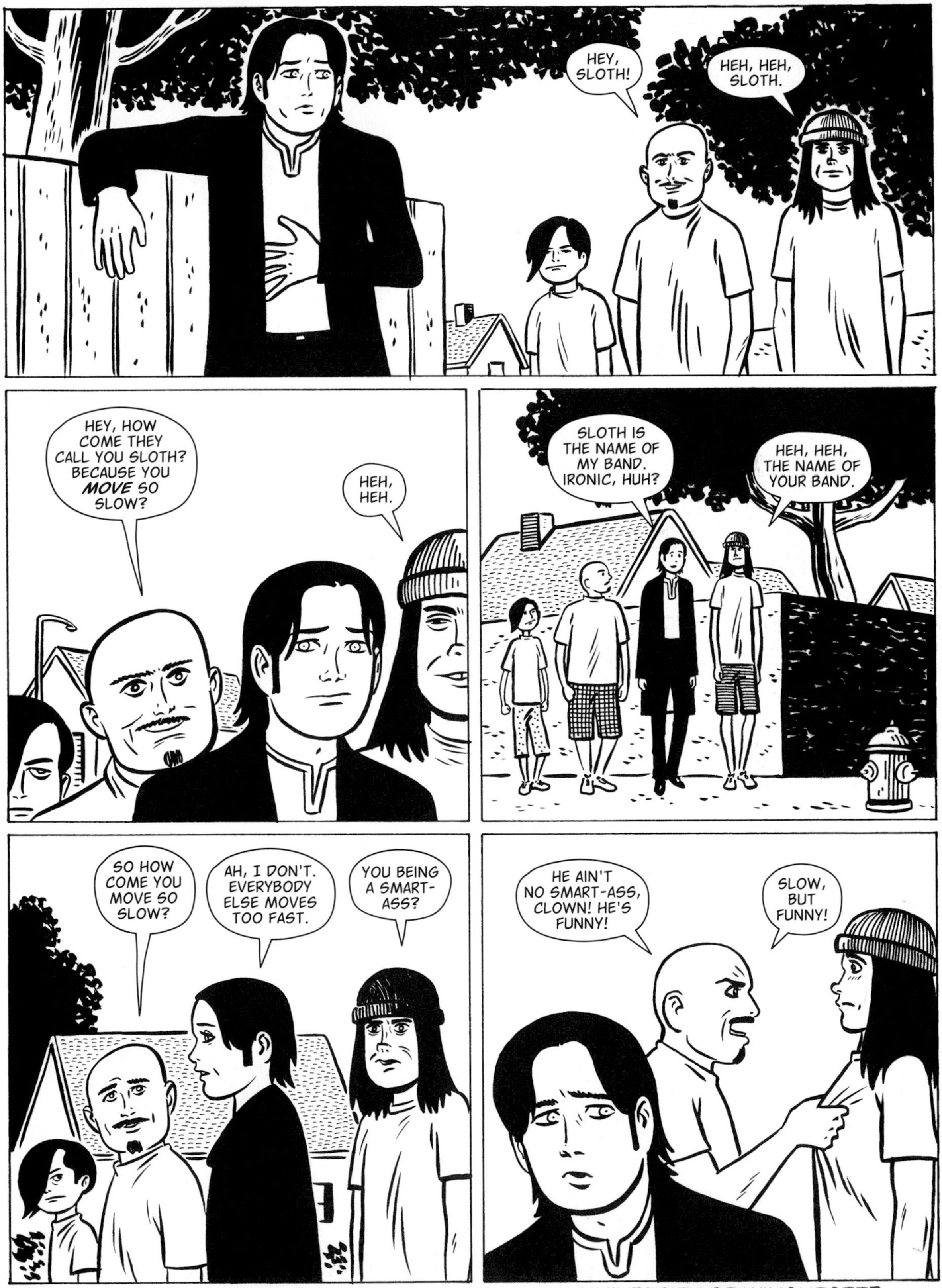
HEY, SLOTH!
HEH, HEH, SLOTH.
HEY, HOW COME THEY CALL YOU SLOTH? BECAUSE YOU *MOVE* SO SLOW?
HEH, HEH.
SLOTH IS THE NAME OF MY BAND. IRONIC, HUH?
HEH, HEH, THE NAME OF YOUR BAND.
SO HOW COME YOU MOVE SO SLOW?
AH, I DON'T. EVERYBODY ELSE MOVES TOO FAST.
YOU BEING A SMART-ASS?
HE AIN'T NO SMART-ASS, CLOWN! HE'S FUNNY!
SLOW, BUT FUNNY!

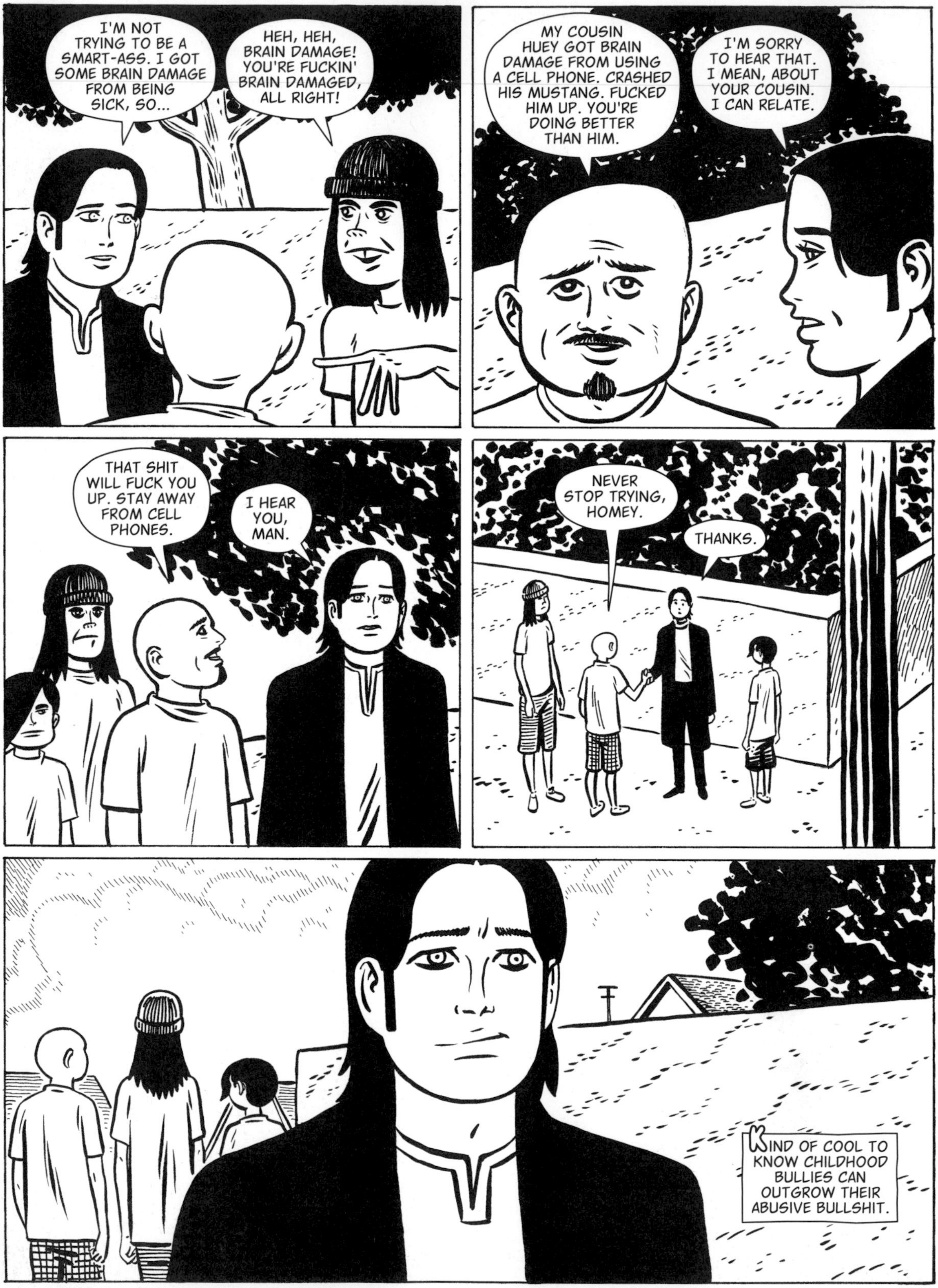
I'M NOT TRYING TO BE A SMART-ASS. I GOT SOME BRAIN DAMAGE FROM BEING SICK, SO...
HEH, HEH, BRAIN DAMAGE! YOU'RE FUCKIN' BRAIN DAMAGED, ALL RIGHT!
MY COUSIN HUEY GOT BRAIN DAMAGE FROM USING A CELL PHONE. CRASHED HIS MUSTANG. FUCKED HIM UP. YOU'RE DOING BETTER THAN HIM.
I'M SORRY TO HEAR THAT. I MEAN, ABOUT YOUR COUSIN. I CAN RELATE.
THAT SHIT WILL FUCK YOU UP. STAY AWAY FROM CELL PHONES.
I HEAR YOU, MAN.
NEVER STOP TRYING, HOMEY.
THANKS.
KIND OF COOL TO KNOW CHILDHOOD BULLIES CAN OUTGROW THEIR ABUSIVE BULLSHIT.

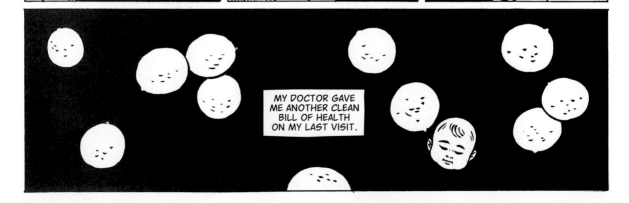

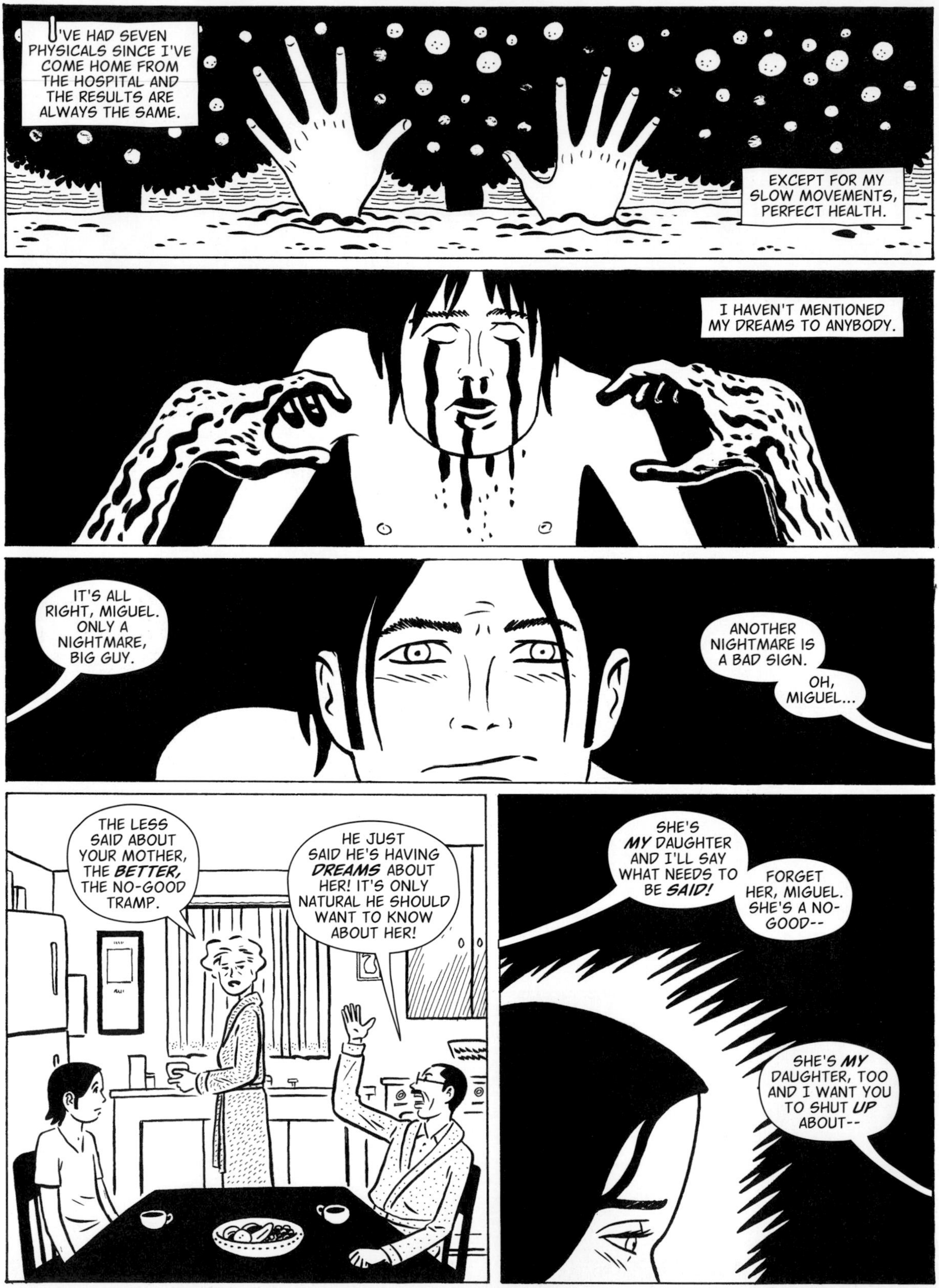
I'VE HAD SEVEN PHYSICALS SINCE I'VE COME HOME FROM THE HOSPITAL AND THE RESULTS ARE ALWAYS THE SAME.
EXCEPT FOR MY SLOW MOVEMENTS, PERFECT HEALTH.
I HAVEN'T MENTIONED MY DREAMS TO ANYBODY.
IT'S ALL RIGHT, MIGUEL. ONLY A NIGHTMARE, BIG GUY.
ANOTHER NIGHTMARE IS A BAD SIGN.
OH, MIGUEL...
THE LESS SAID ABOUT YOUR MOTHER, THE BETTER, THE NO-GOOD TRAMP.
HE JUST SAID HE'S HAVING DREAMS ABOUT HER! IT'S ONLY NATURAL HE SHOULD WANT TO KNOW ABOUT HER!
SHE'S MY DAUGHTER AND I'LL SAY WHAT NEEDS TO BE SAID!
FORGET HER, MIGUEL. SHE'S A NO-GOOD--
SHE'S MY DAUGHTER, TOO AND I WANT YOU TO SHUT UP ABOUT--

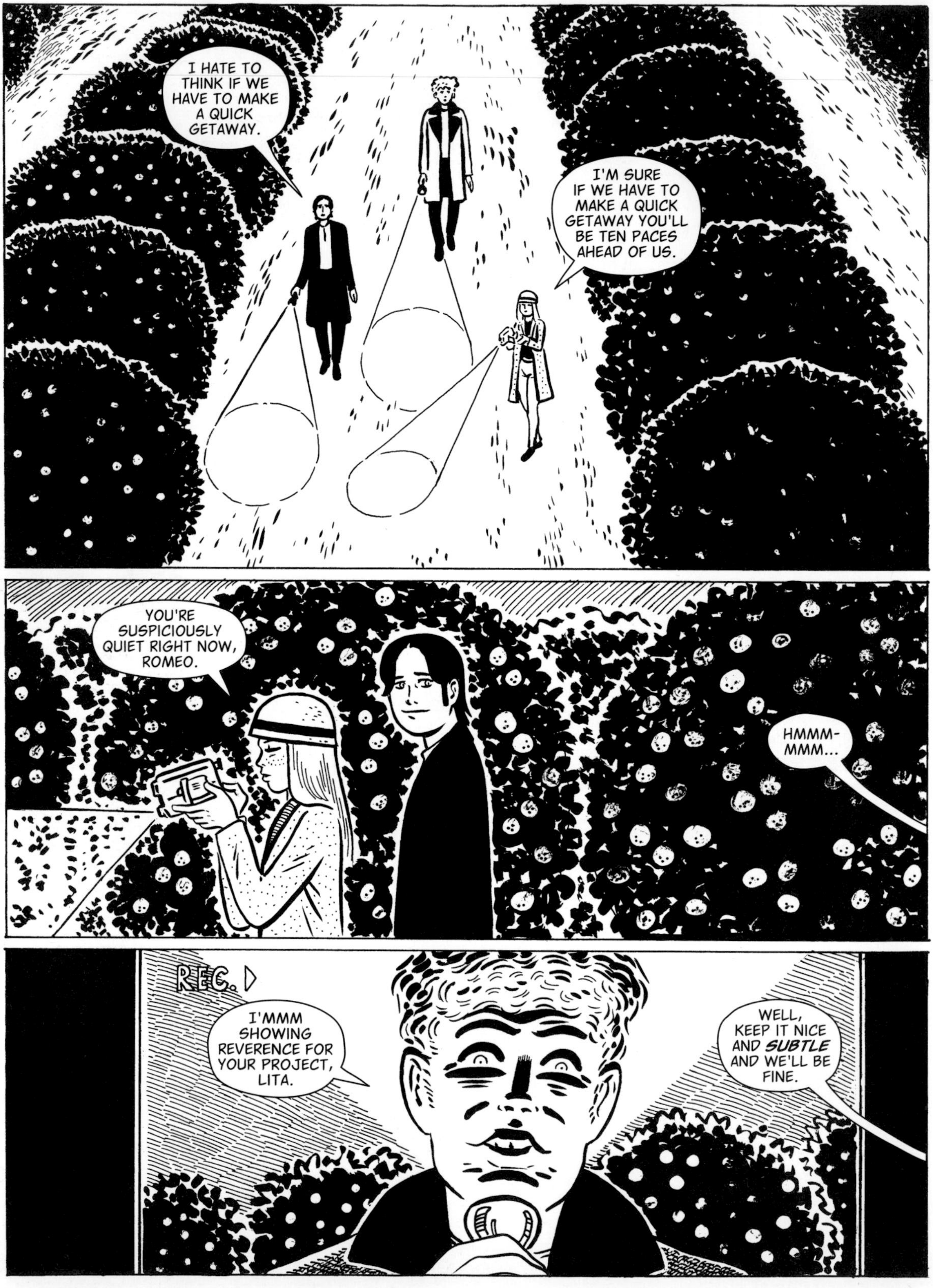

I HATE TO THINK IF WE HAVE TO MAKE A QUICK GETAWAY.
I'M SURE IF WE HAVE TO MAKE A QUICK GETAWAY YOU'LL BE TEN PACES AHEAD OF US.
YOU'RE SUSPICIOUSLY QUIET RIGHT NOW, ROMEO.
HMMM-MMM...
REC.
I'MMM SHOWING REVERENCE FOR YOUR PROJECT, LITA.
WELL, KEEP IT NICE AND SUBTLE AND WE'LL BE FINE.

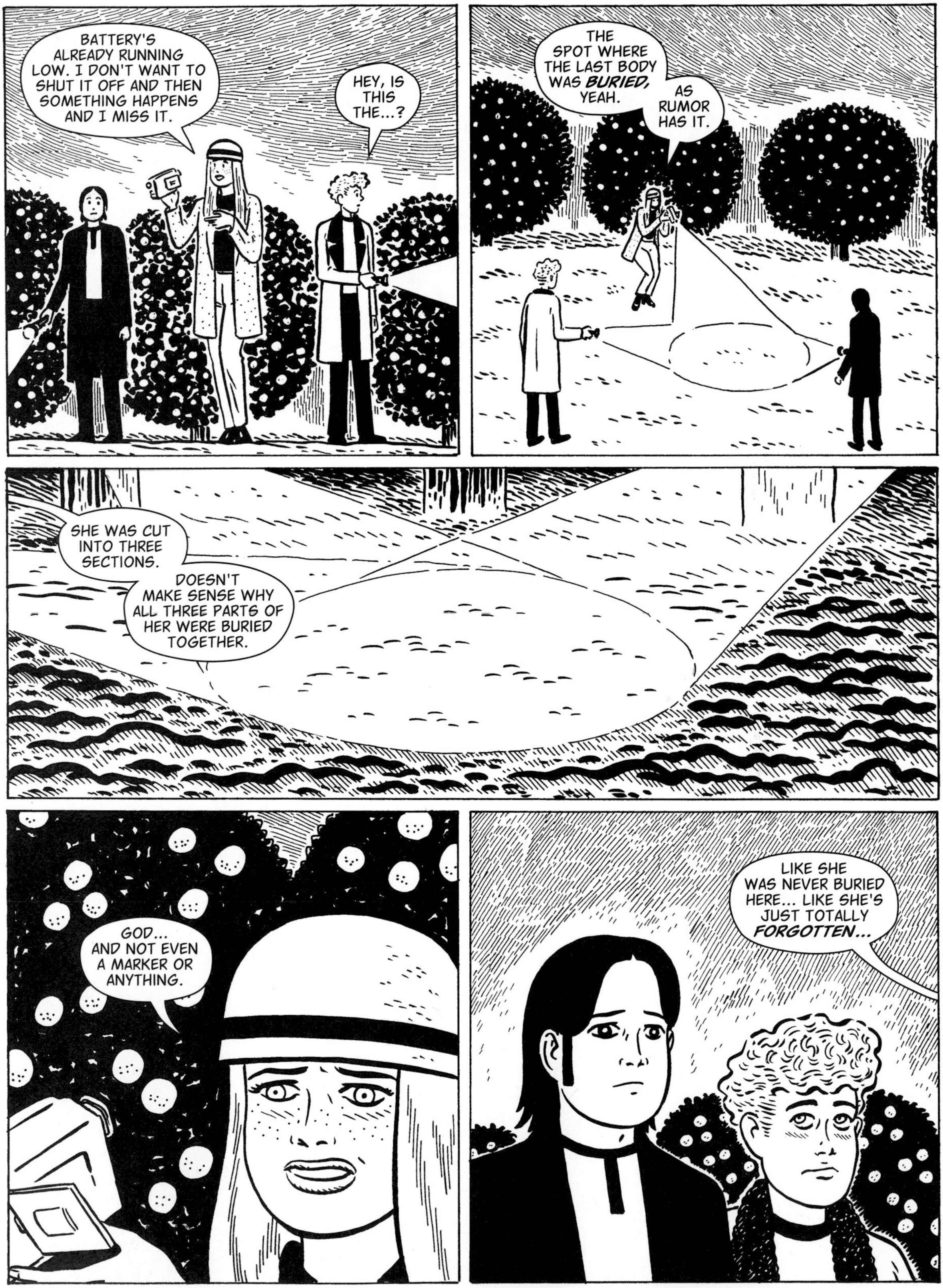
BATTERY'S ALREADY RUNNING LOW. I DON'T WANT TO SHUT IT OFF AND THEN SOMETHING HAPPENS AND I MISS IT.
HEY, IS THIS THE...?
THE SPOT WHERE THE LAST BODY WAS *BURIED,* YEAH.
AS RUMOR HAS IT.
SHE WAS CUT INTO THREE SECTIONS.
DOESN'T MAKE SENSE WHY ALL THREE PARTS OF HER WERE BURIED TOGETHER.
GOD... AND NOT EVEN A MARKER OR ANYTHING.
LIKE SHE WAS NEVER BURIED HERE... LIKE SHE'S JUST TOTALLY *FORGOTTEN...*

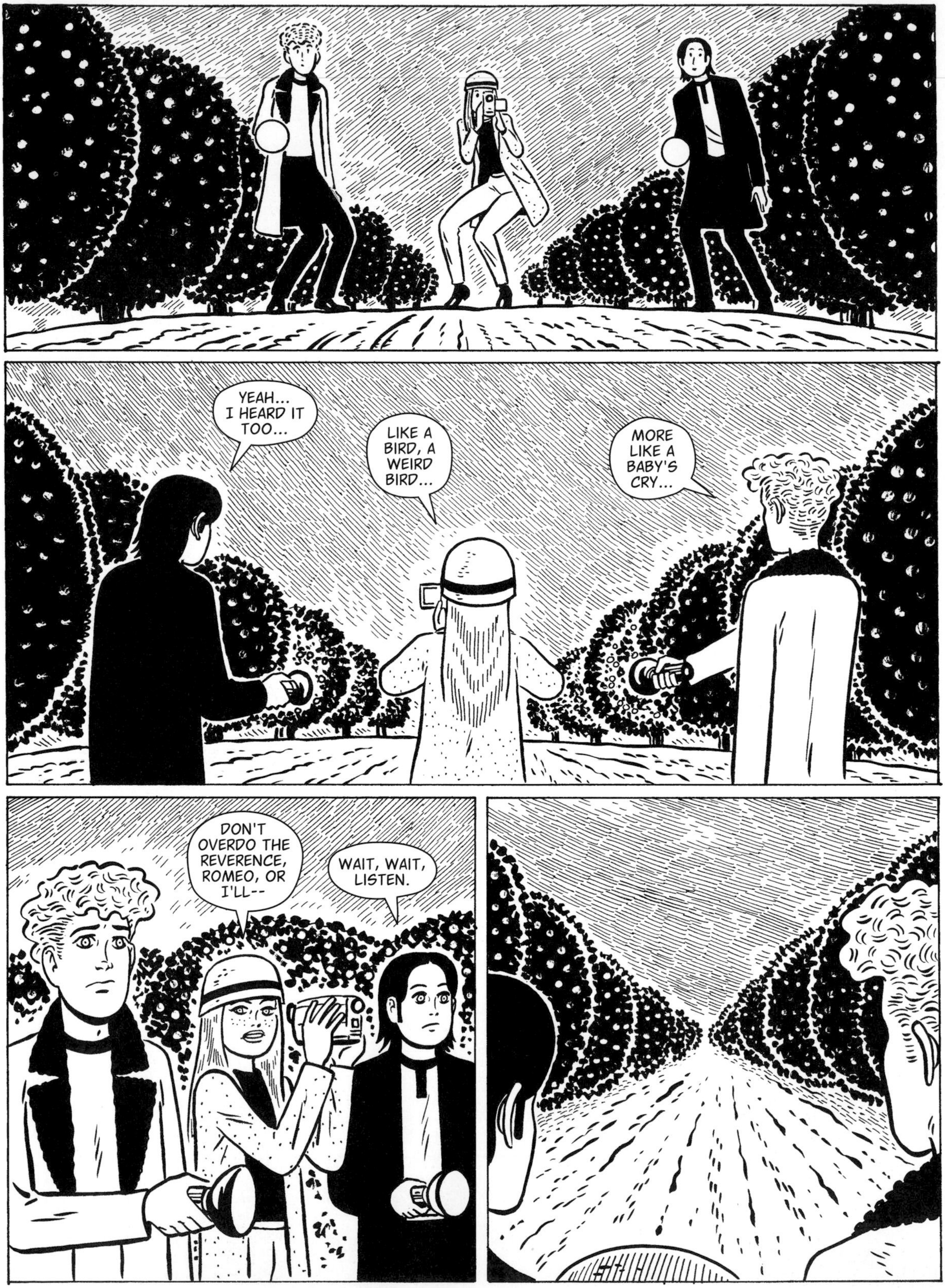
YEAH... I HEARD IT TOO...
LIKE A BIRD, A WEIRD BIRD...
MORE LIKE A BABY'S CRY...
DON'T OVERDO THE REVERENCE, ROMEO, OR I'LL--
WAIT, WAIT, LISTEN.

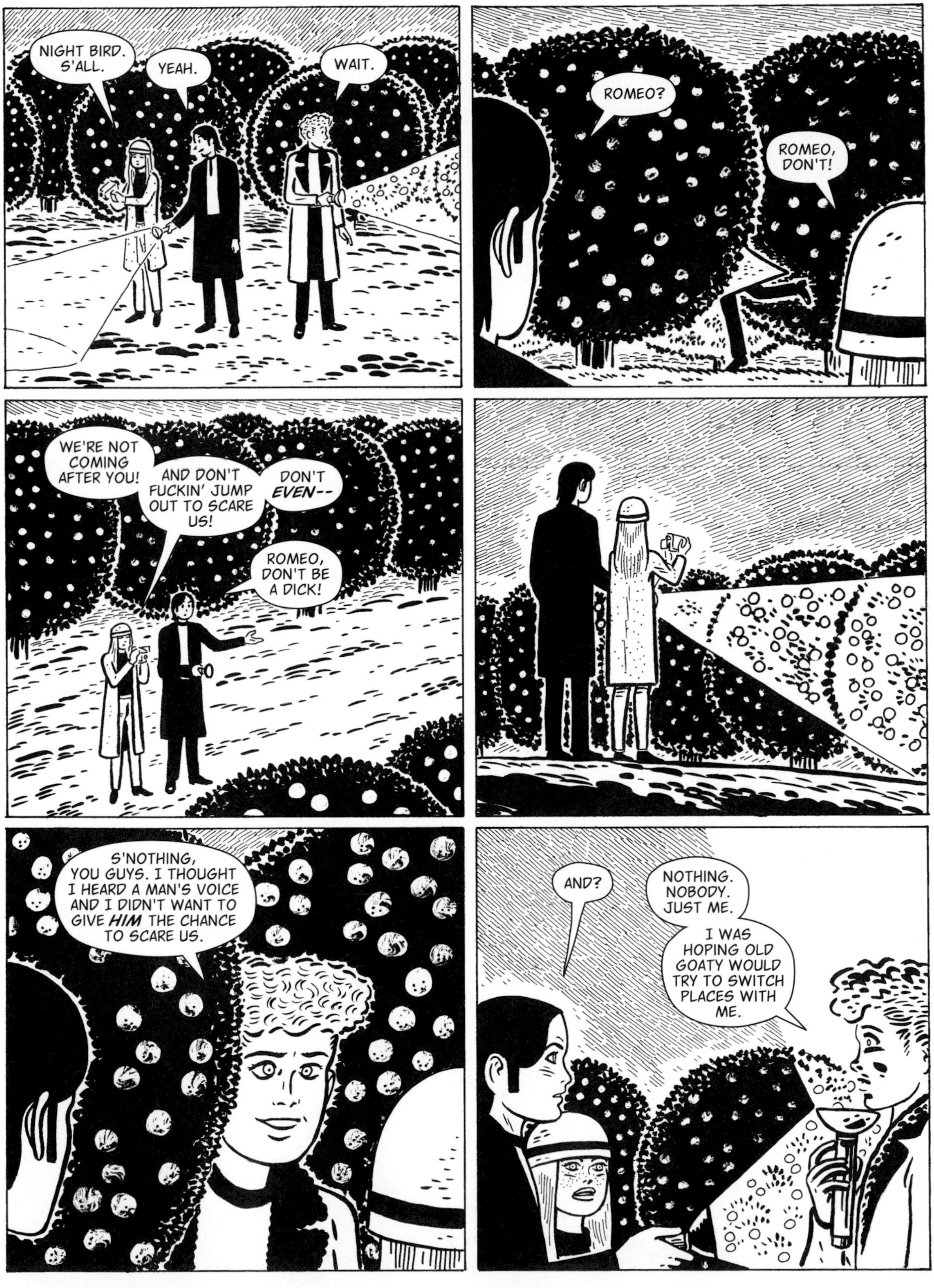
NIGHT BIRD. S'ALL.
YEAH.
WAIT.
ROMEO?
ROMEO, DON'T!
WE'RE NOT COMING AFTER YOU!
AND DON'T FUCKIN' JUMP OUT TO SCARE US!
DON'T *EVEN--*
ROMEO, DON'T BE A DICK!
S'NOTHING, YOU GUYS. I THOUGHT I HEARD A MAN'S VOICE AND I DIDN'T WANT TO GIVE *HIM* THE CHANCE TO SCARE US.
AND?
NOTHING. NOBODY. JUST ME.
I WAS HOPING OLD GOATY WOULD TRY TO SWITCH PLACES WITH ME.

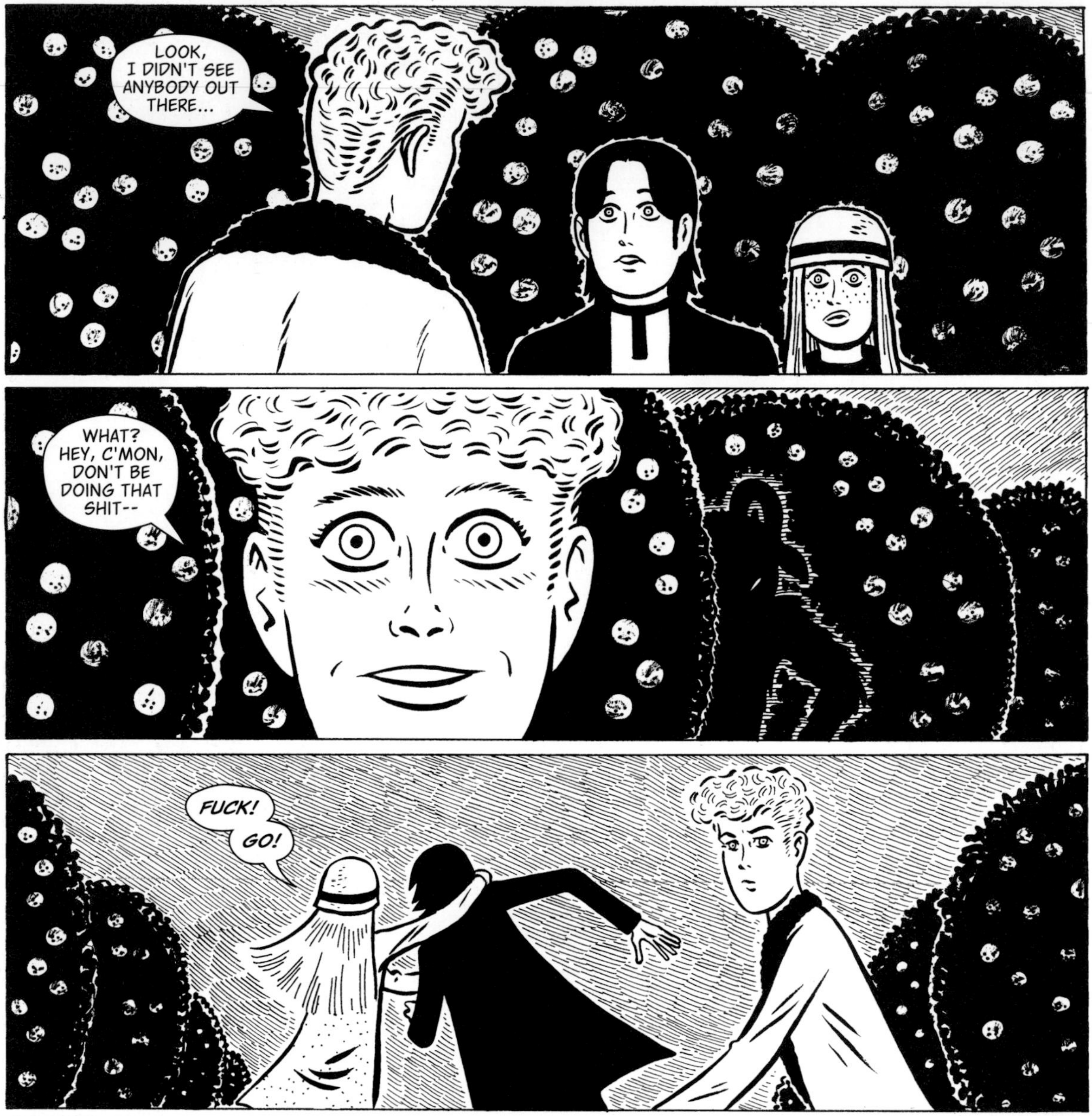
LOOK, I DIDN'T SEE ANYBODY OUT THERE...
WHAT? HEY, C'MON, DON'T BE DOING THAT SHIT--
FUCK!
GO!
ROMEO...!

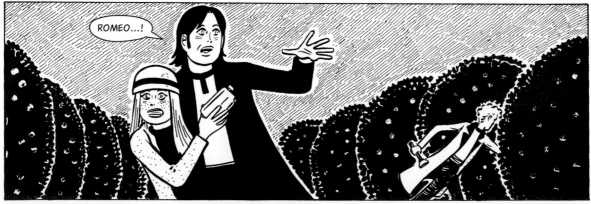

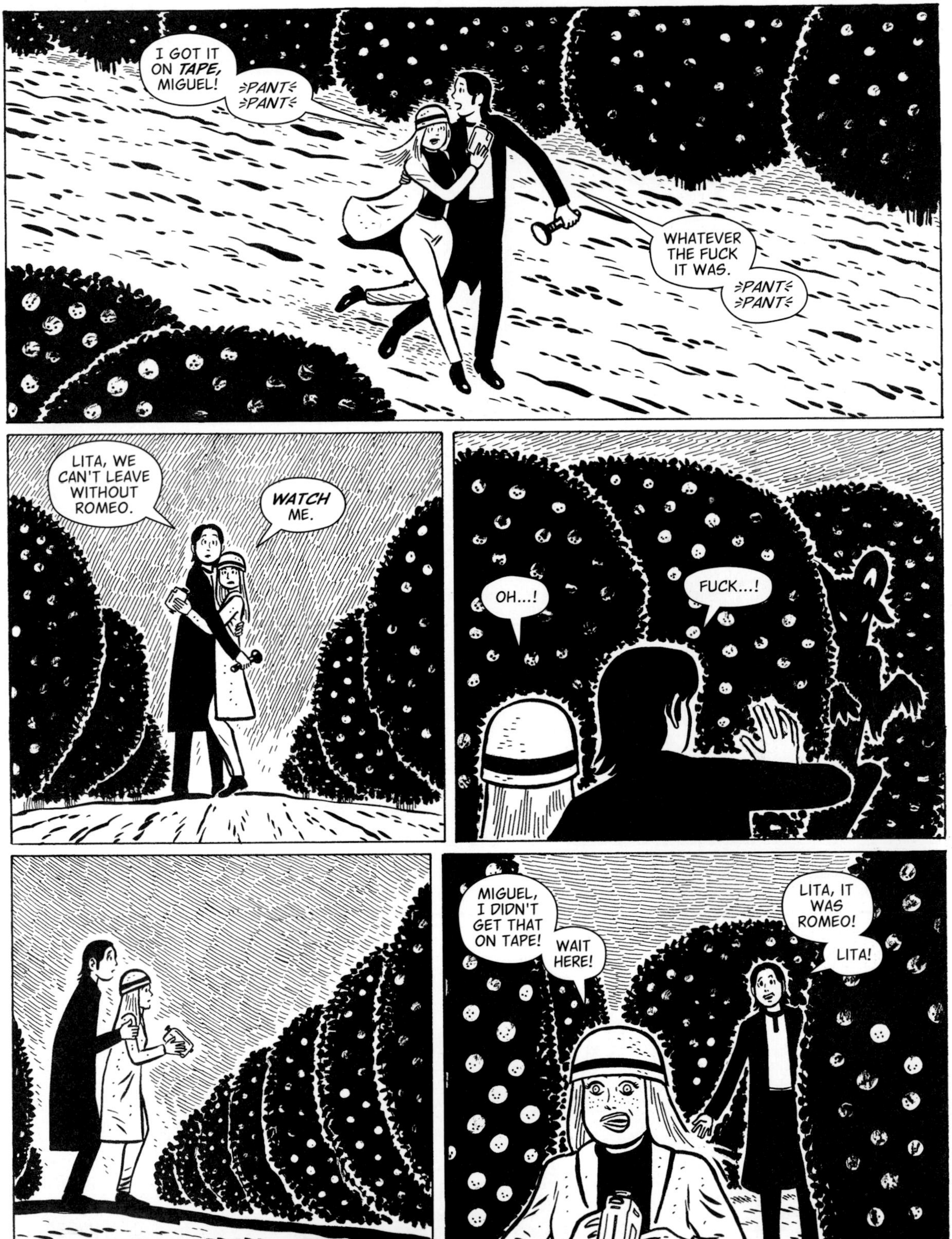
I GOT IT ON *TAPE,* MIGUEL!
PANT PANT
WHATEVER THE FUCK IT WAS.
PANT PANT
LITA, WE CAN'T LEAVE WITHOUT ROMEO.
WATCH ME.
OH...!
FUCK...!
MIGUEL, I DIDN'T GET THAT ON TAPE!
WAIT HERE!
LITA, IT WAS ROMEO!
LITA!

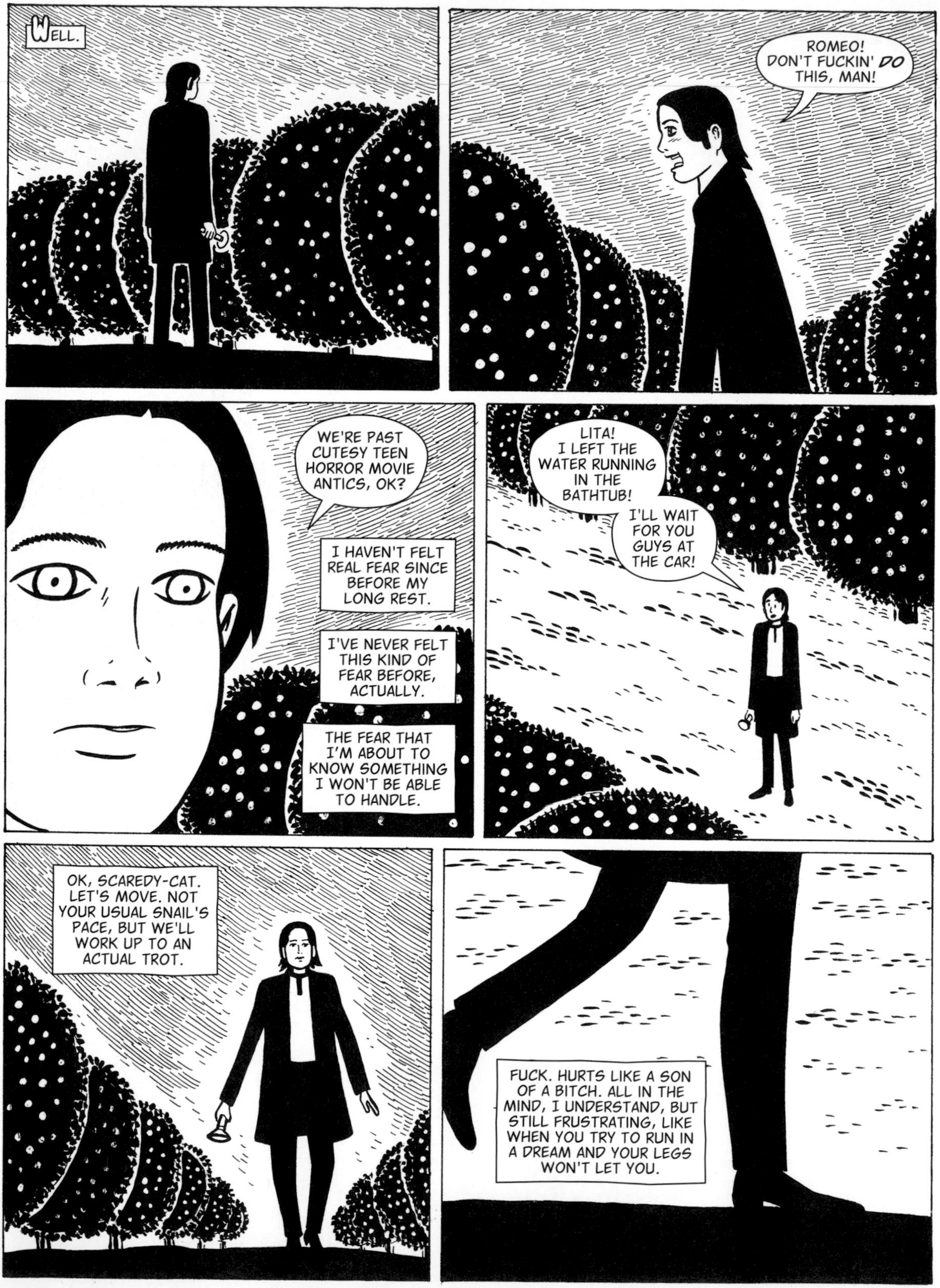
WELL.
ROMEO! DON'T FUCKIN' DO THIS, MAN!
WE'RE PAST CUTESY TEEN HORROR MOVIE ANTICS, OK?
I HAVEN'T FELT REAL FEAR SINCE BEFORE MY LONG REST.
I'VE NEVER FELT THIS KIND OF FEAR BEFORE, ACTUALLY.
THE FEAR THAT I'M ABOUT TO KNOW SOMETHING I WON'T BE ABLE TO HANDLE.
LITA! I LEFT THE WATER RUNNING IN THE BATHTUB!
I'LL WAIT FOR YOU GUYS AT THE CAR!
OK, SCAREDY-CAT. LET'S MOVE. NOT YOUR USUAL SNAIL'S PACE, BUT WE'LL WORK UP TO AN ACTUAL TROT.
FUCK. HURTS LIKE A SON OF A BITCH. ALL IN THE MIND, I UNDERSTAND, BUT STILL FRUSTRATING, LIKE WHEN YOU TRY TO RUN IN A DREAM AND YOUR LEGS WON'T LET YOU.

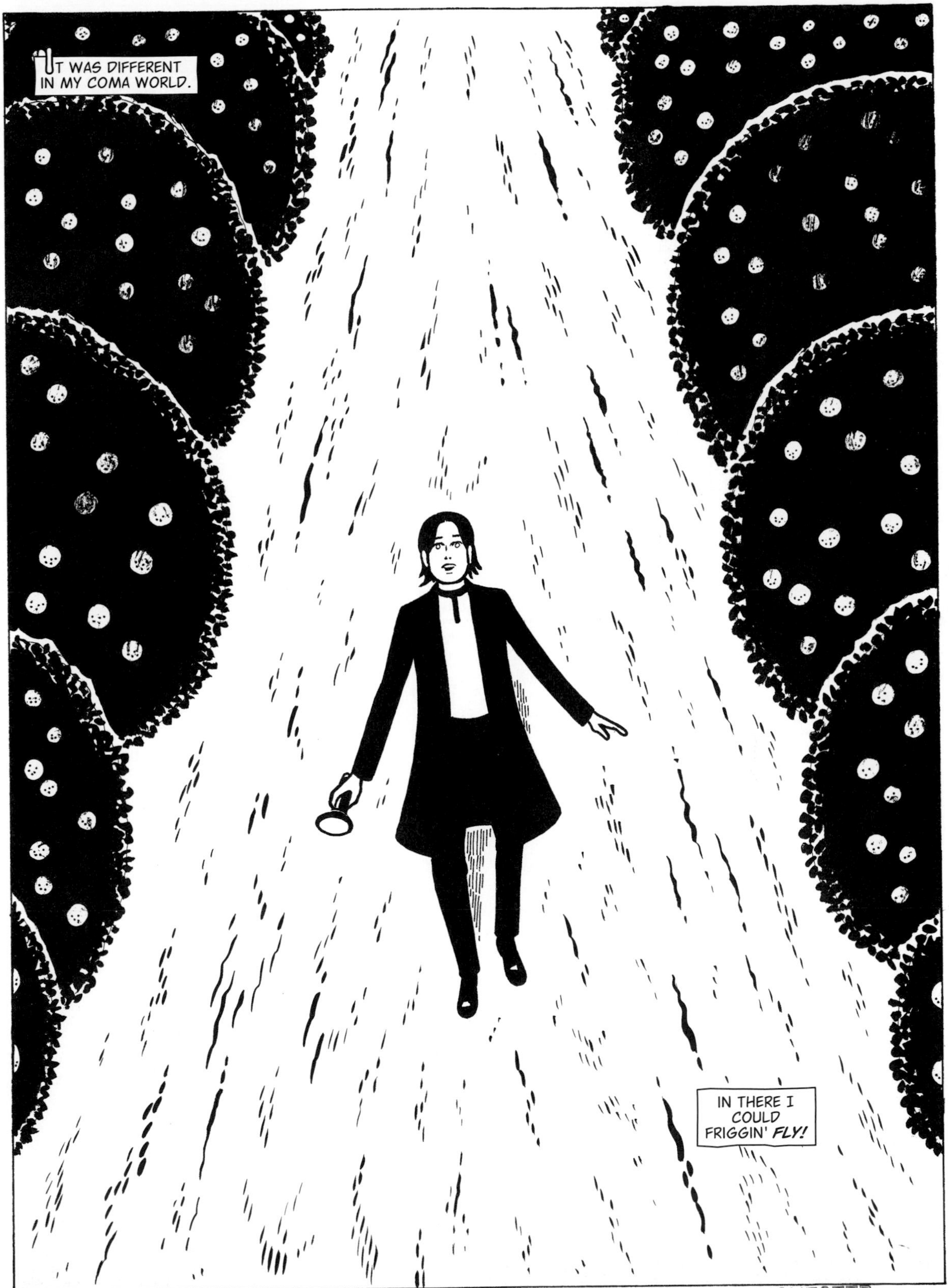
IT WAS DIFFERENT IN MY COMA WORLD.
IN THERE I COULD FRIGGIN' FLY!

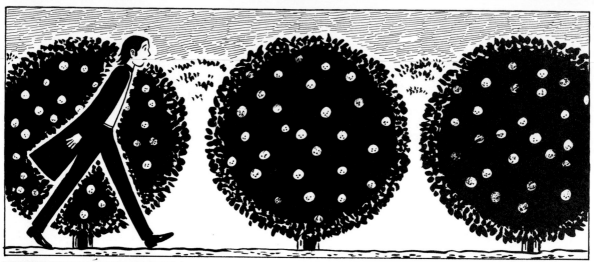

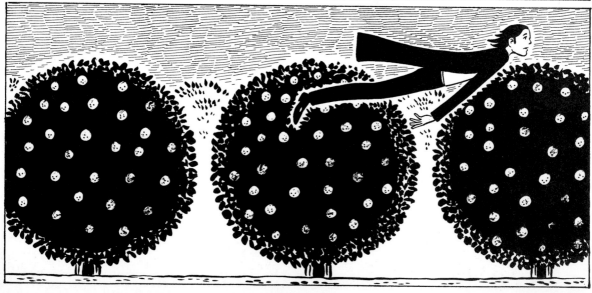

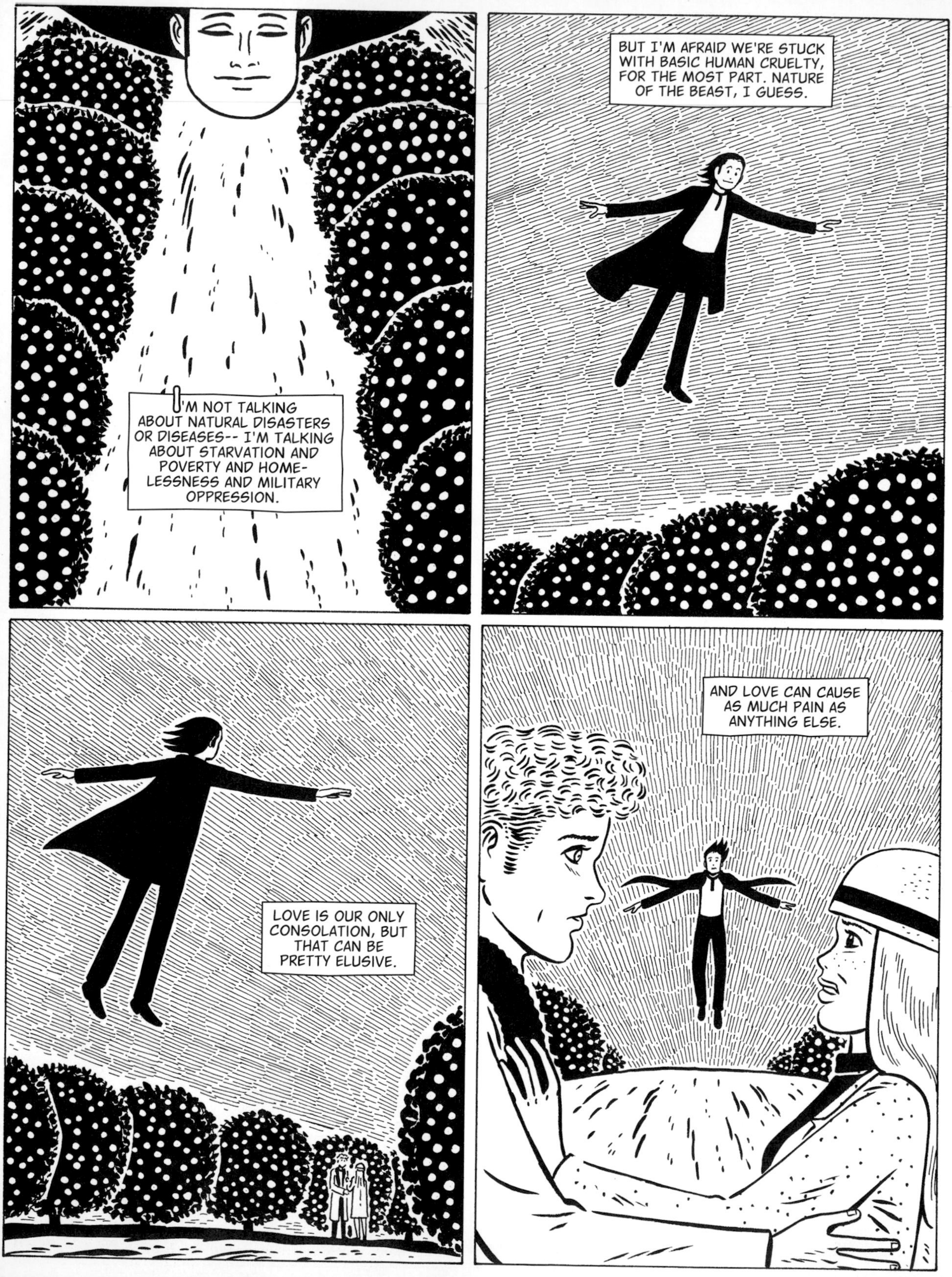
I'M NOT TALKING ABOUT NATURAL DISASTERS OR DISEASES-- I'M TALKING ABOUT STARVATION AND POVERTY AND HOMELESSNESS AND MILITARY OPPRESSION.
BUT I'M AFRAID WE'RE STUCK WITH BASIC HUMAN CRUELTY, FOR THE MOST PART. NATURE OF THE BEAST, I GUESS.
LOVE IS OUR ONLY CONSOLATION, BUT THAT CAN BE PRETTY ELUSIVE.
AND LOVE CAN CAUSE AS MUCH PAIN AS ANYTHING ELSE.

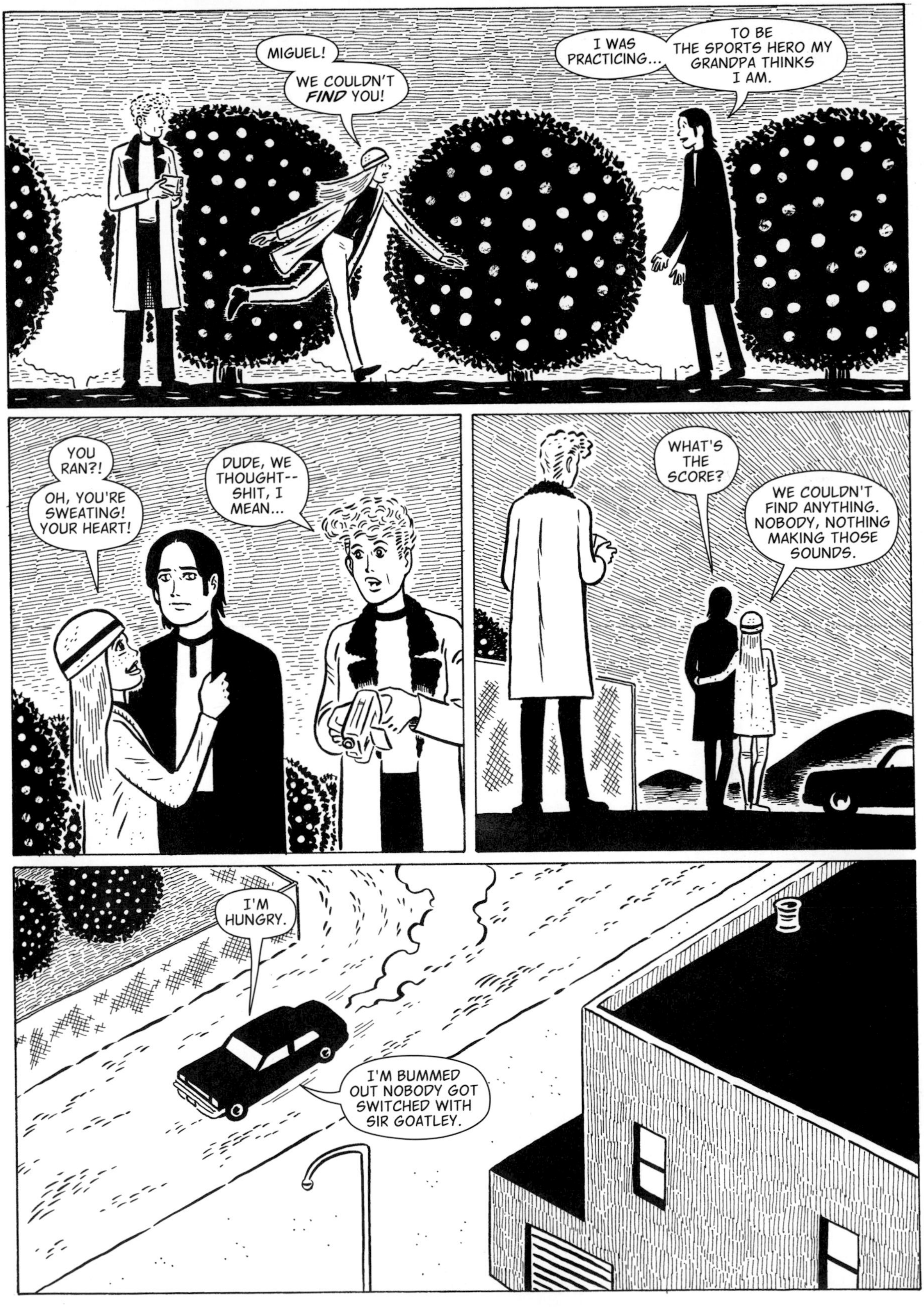

MIGUEL!
WE COULDN'T *FIND* YOU!
I WAS PRACTICING...
TO BE THE SPORTS HERO MY GRANDPA THINKS I AM.
YOU RAN?!
OH, YOU'RE SWEATING! YOUR HEART!
DUDE, WE THOUGHT-- SHIT, I MEAN...
WHAT'S THE SCORE?
WE COULDN'T FIND ANYTHING. NOBODY, NOTHING MAKING THOSE SOUNDS.
I'M HUNGRY.
I'M BUMMED OUT NOBODY GOT SWITCHED WITH SIR GOATLEY.

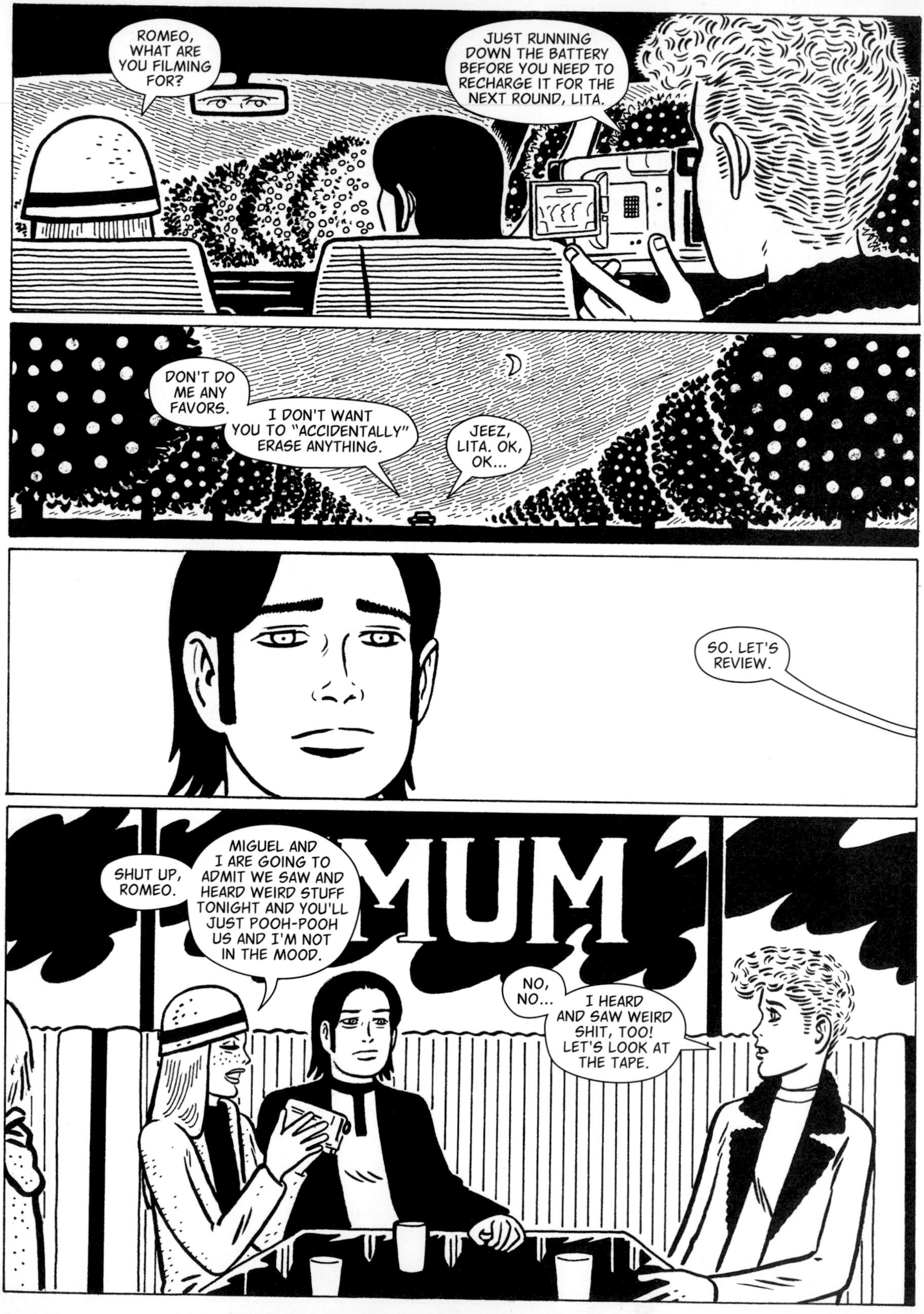
ROMEO, WHAT ARE YOU FILMING FOR?
JUST RUNNING DOWN THE BATTERY BEFORE YOU NEED TO RECHARGE IT FOR THE NEXT ROUND, LITA.
DON'T DO ME ANY FAVORS.
I DON'T WANT YOU TO "ACCIDENTALLY" ERASE ANYTHING.
JEEZ, LITA. OK, OK...
SO. LET'S REVIEW.
MUM
SHUT UP, ROMEO.
MIGUEL AND I ARE GOING TO ADMIT WE SAW AND HEARD WEIRD STUFF TONIGHT AND YOU'LL JUST POOH-POOH US AND I'M NOT IN THE MOOD.
NO, NO...
I HEARD AND SAW WEIRD SHIT, TOO! LET'S LOOK AT THE TAPE.

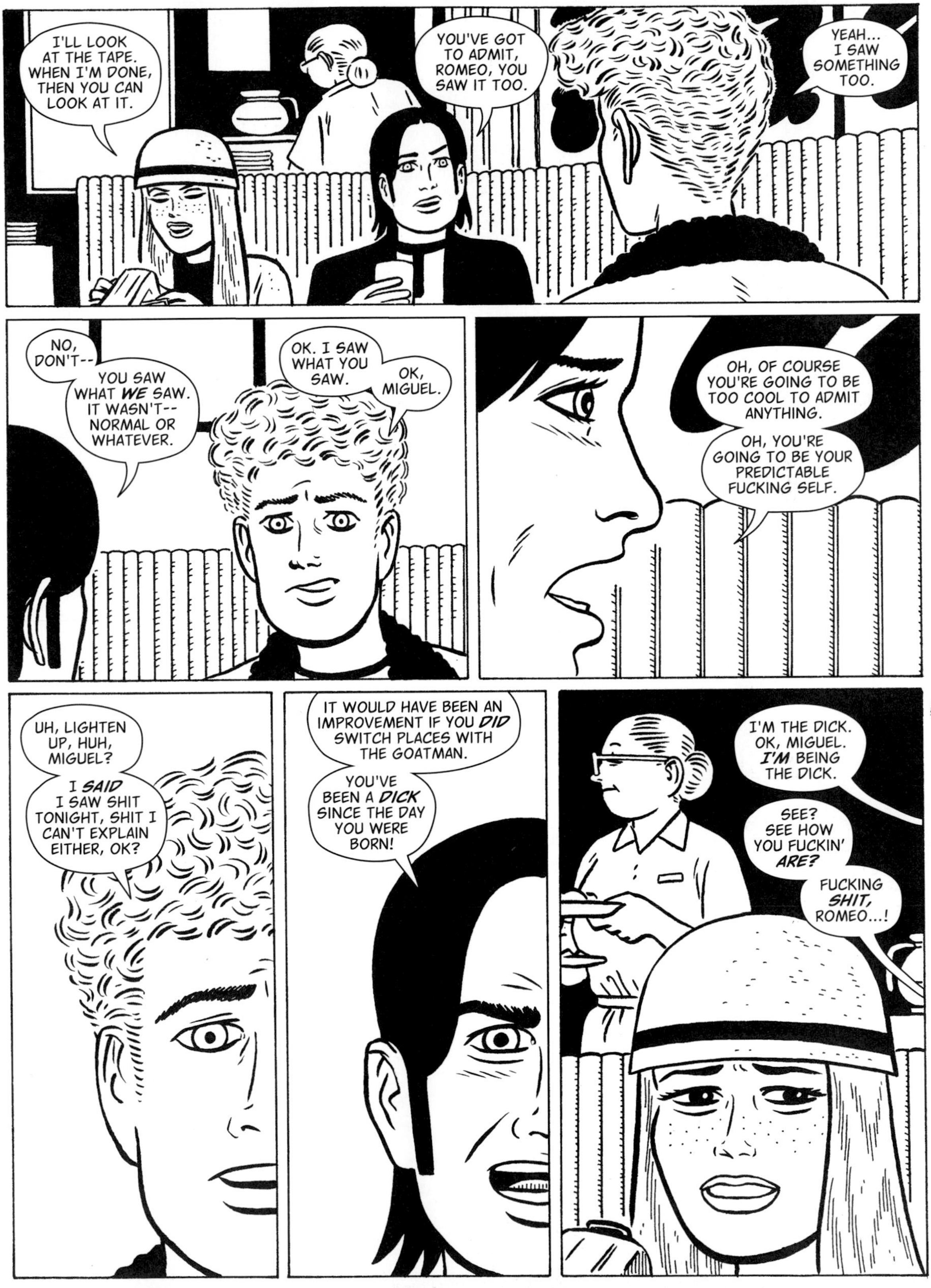

I'LL LOOK AT THE TAPE. WHEN I'M DONE, THEN YOU CAN LOOK AT IT.
YOU'VE GOT TO ADMIT, ROMEO, YOU SAW IT TOO.
YEAH... I SAW SOMETHING TOO.
NO, DON'T--
YOU SAW WHAT *WE* SAW. IT WASN'T-- NORMAL OR WHATEVER.
OK. I SAW WHAT YOU SAW.
OK, MIGUEL.
OH, OF COURSE YOU'RE GOING TO BE TOO COOL TO ADMIT ANYTHING.
OH, YOU'RE GOING TO BE YOUR PREDICTABLE FUCKING SELF.
UH, LIGHTEN UP, HUH, MIGUEL?
I *SAID* I SAW SHIT TONIGHT, SHIT I CAN'T EXPLAIN EITHER, OK?
IT WOULD HAVE BEEN AN IMPROVEMENT IF YOU *DID* SWITCH PLACES WITH THE GOATMAN.
YOU'VE BEEN A *DICK* SINCE THE DAY YOU WERE BORN!
I'M THE DICK. OK, MIGUEL. *I'M* BEING THE DICK.
SEE? SEE HOW YOU FUCKIN' *ARE?*
FUCKING *SHIT,* ROMEO...!

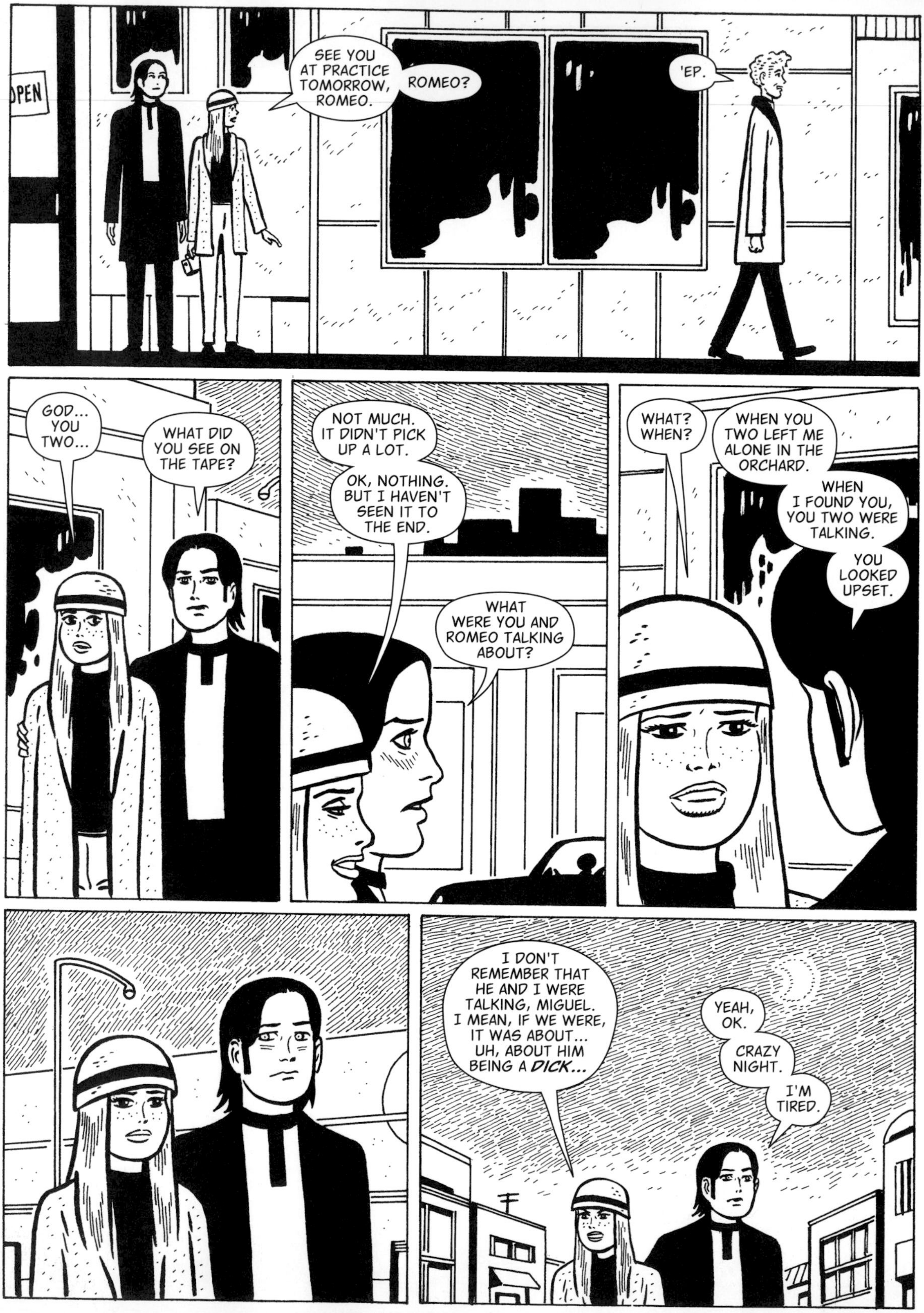
OPEN
SEE YOU AT PRACTICE TOMORROW, ROMEO.
ROMEO?
'EP.
GOD... YOU TWO...
WHAT DID YOU SEE ON THE TAPE?
NOT MUCH. IT DIDN'T PICK UP A LOT.
OK, NOTHING. BUT I HAVEN'T SEEN IT TO THE END.
WHAT WERE YOU AND ROMEO TALKING ABOUT?
WHAT? WHEN?
WHEN YOU TWO LEFT ME ALONE IN THE ORCHARD.
WHEN I FOUND YOU, YOU TWO WERE TALKING.
YOU LOOKED UPSET.
I DON'T REMEMBER THAT HE AND I WERE TALKING, MIGUEL. I MEAN, IF WE WERE, IT WAS ABOUT... UH, ABOUT HIM BEING A ***DICK...***
YEAH, OK.
CRAZY NIGHT.
I'M TIRED.

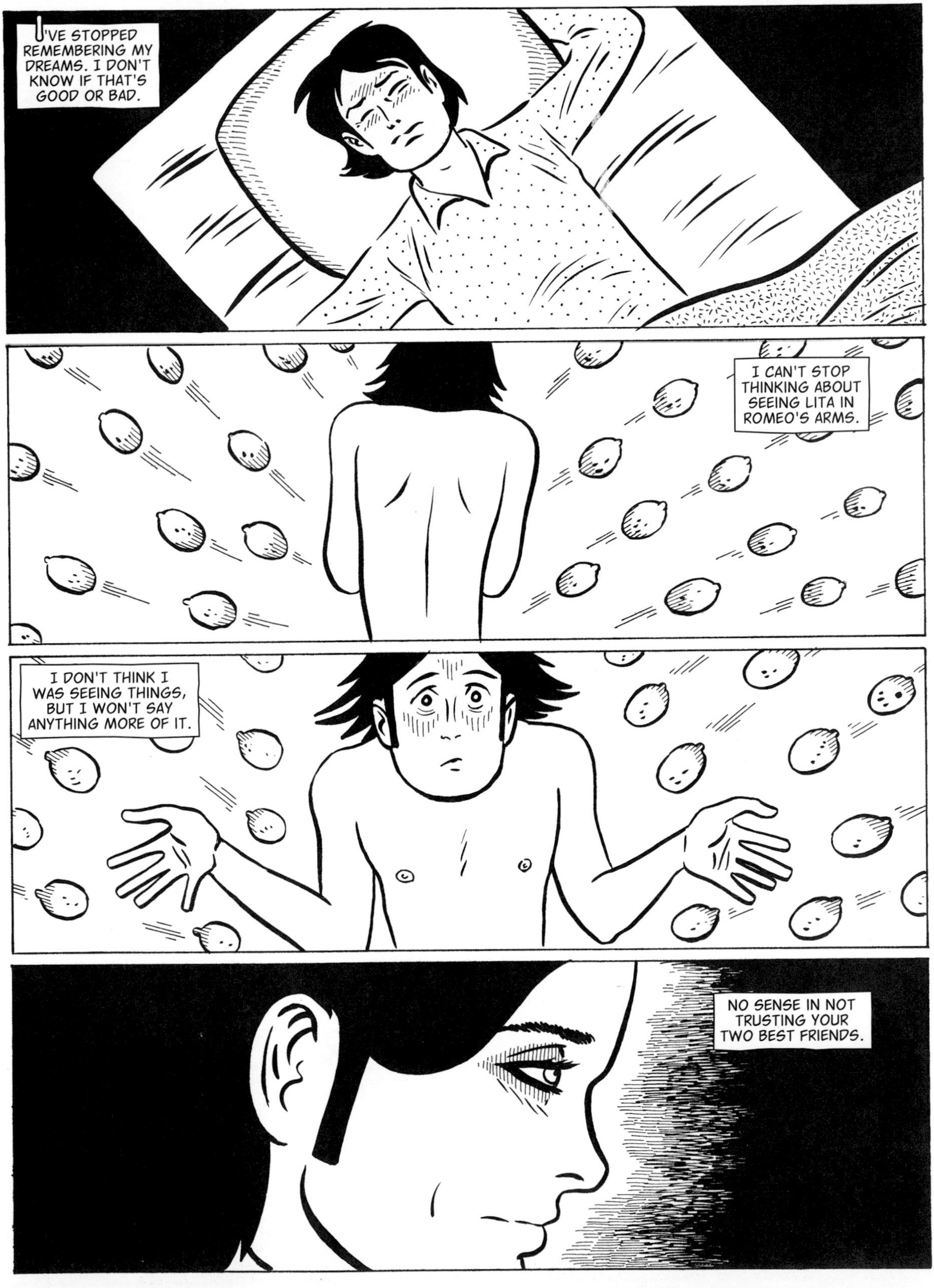
I'VE STOPPED REMEMBERING MY DREAMS. I DON'T KNOW IF THAT'S GOOD OR BAD.
I CAN'T STOP THINKING ABOUT SEEING LITA IN ROMEO'S ARMS.
I DON'T THINK I WAS SEEING THINGS, BUT I WON'T SAY ANYTHING MORE OF IT.
NO SENSE IN NOT TRUSTING YOUR TWO BEST FRIENDS.

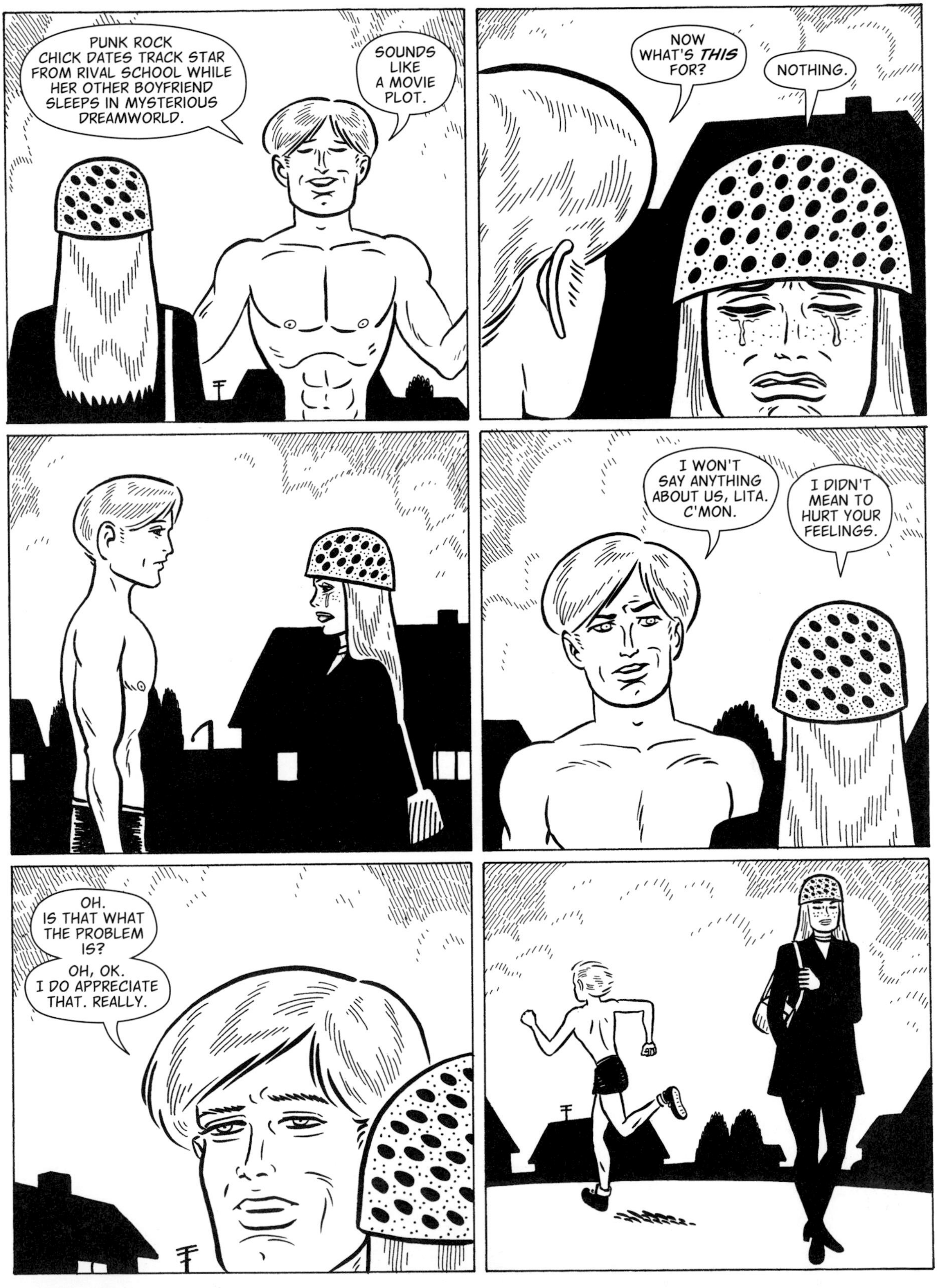
PUNK ROCK CHICK DATES TRACK STAR FROM RIVAL SCHOOL WHILE HER OTHER BOYFRIEND SLEEPS IN MYSTERIOUS DREAMWORLD.
SOUNDS LIKE A MOVIE PLOT.
NOW WHAT'S *THIS* FOR?
NOTHING.
I WON'T SAY ANYTHING ABOUT US, LITA. C'MON.
I DIDN'T MEAN TO HURT YOUR FEELINGS.
OH. IS THAT WHAT THE PROBLEM IS?
OH, OK. I DO APPRECIATE THAT. REALLY.

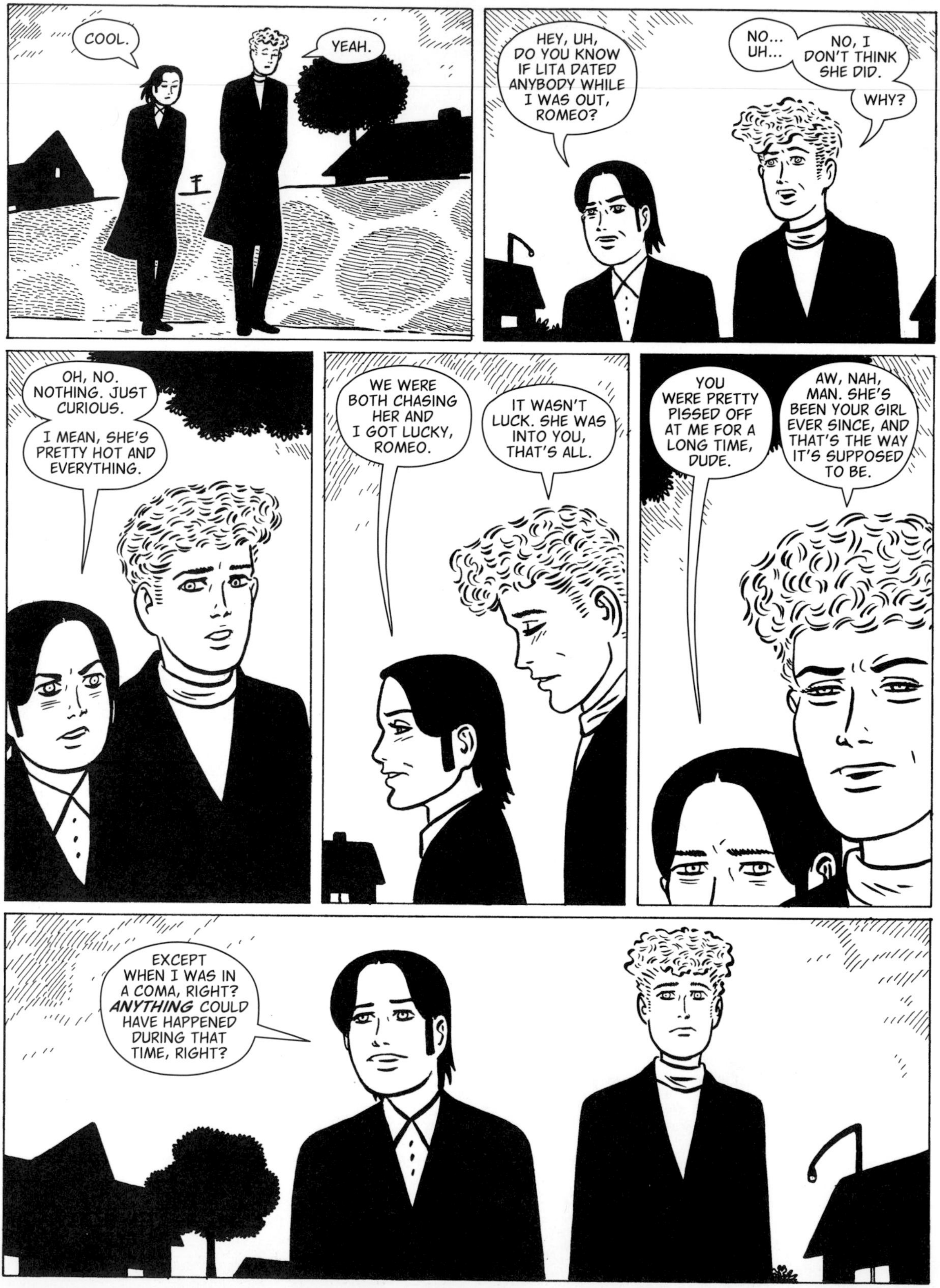
COOL.
YEAH.
HEY, UH, DO YOU KNOW IF LITA DATED ANYBODY WHILE I WAS OUT, ROMEO?
NO... UH...
NO, I DON'T THINK SHE DID.
WHY?
OH, NO. NOTHING. JUST CURIOUS.
I MEAN, SHE'S PRETTY HOT AND EVERYTHING.
WE WERE BOTH CHASING HER AND I GOT LUCKY, ROMEO.
IT WASN'T LUCK. SHE WAS INTO YOU, THAT'S ALL.
YOU WERE PRETTY PISSED OFF AT ME FOR A LONG TIME, DUDE.
AW, NAH, MAN. SHE'S BEEN YOUR GIRL EVER SINCE, AND THAT'S THE WAY IT'S SUPPOSED TO BE.
EXCEPT WHEN I WAS IN A COMA, RIGHT? ***ANYTHING*** COULD HAVE HAPPENED DURING THAT TIME, RIGHT?

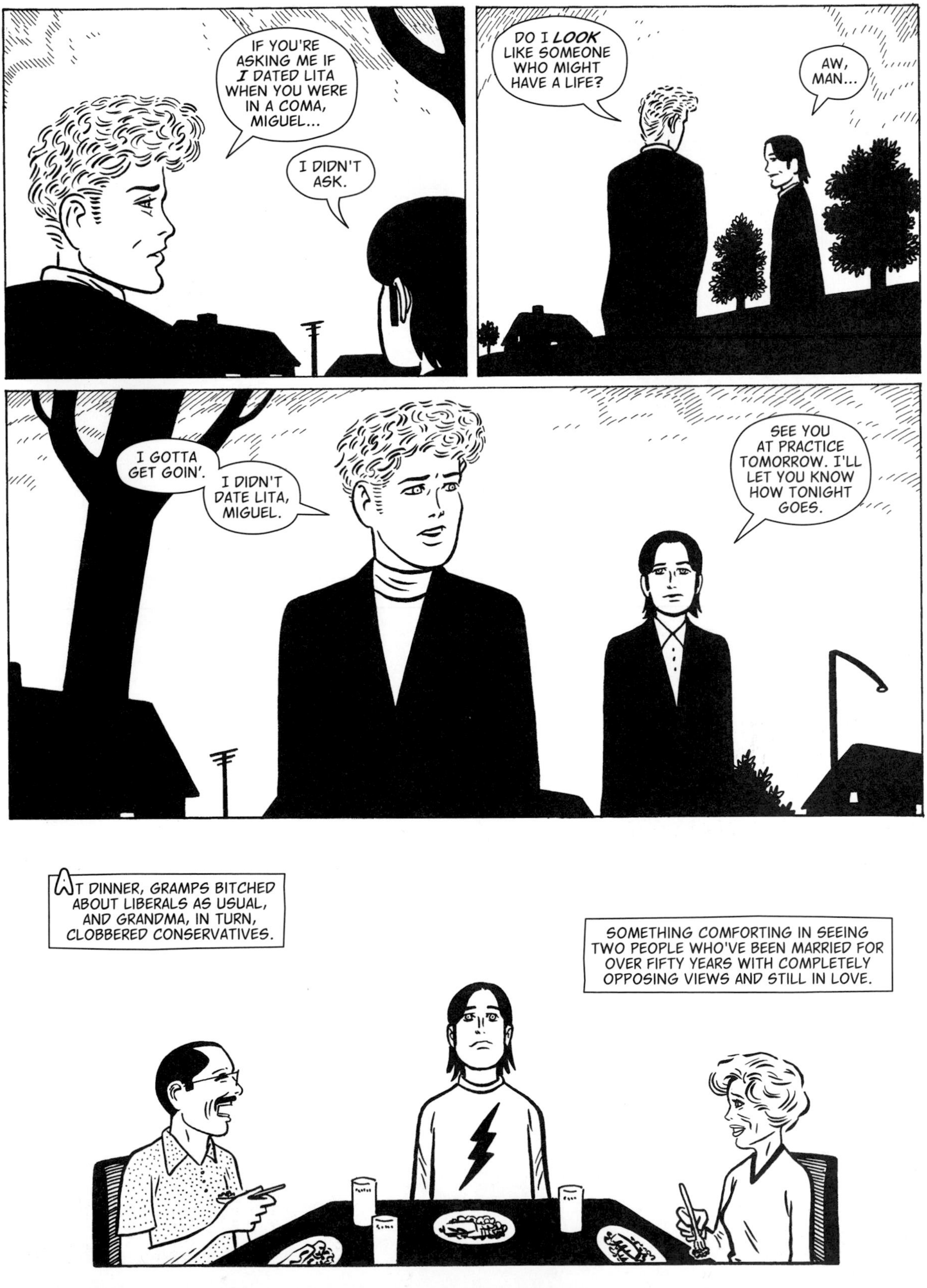
IF YOU'RE ASKING ME IF *I* DATED LITA WHEN YOU WERE IN A COMA, MIGUEL...
I DIDN'T ASK.
DO I **LOOK** LIKE SOMEONE WHO MIGHT HAVE A LIFE?
AW, MAN...
I GOTTA GET GOIN'.
I DIDN'T DATE LITA, MIGUEL.
SEE YOU AT PRACTICE TOMORROW. I'LL LET YOU KNOW HOW TONIGHT GOES.
AT DINNER, GRAMPS BITCHED ABOUT LIBERALS AS USUAL, AND GRANDMA, IN TURN, CLOBBERED CONSERVATIVES.
SOMETHING COMFORTING IN SEEING TWO PEOPLE WHO'VE BEEN MARRIED FOR OVER FIFTY YEARS WITH COMPLETELY OPPOSING VIEWS AND STILL IN LOVE.

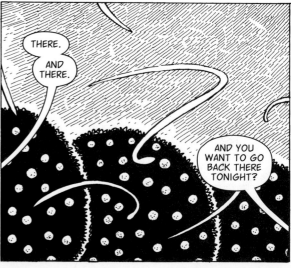

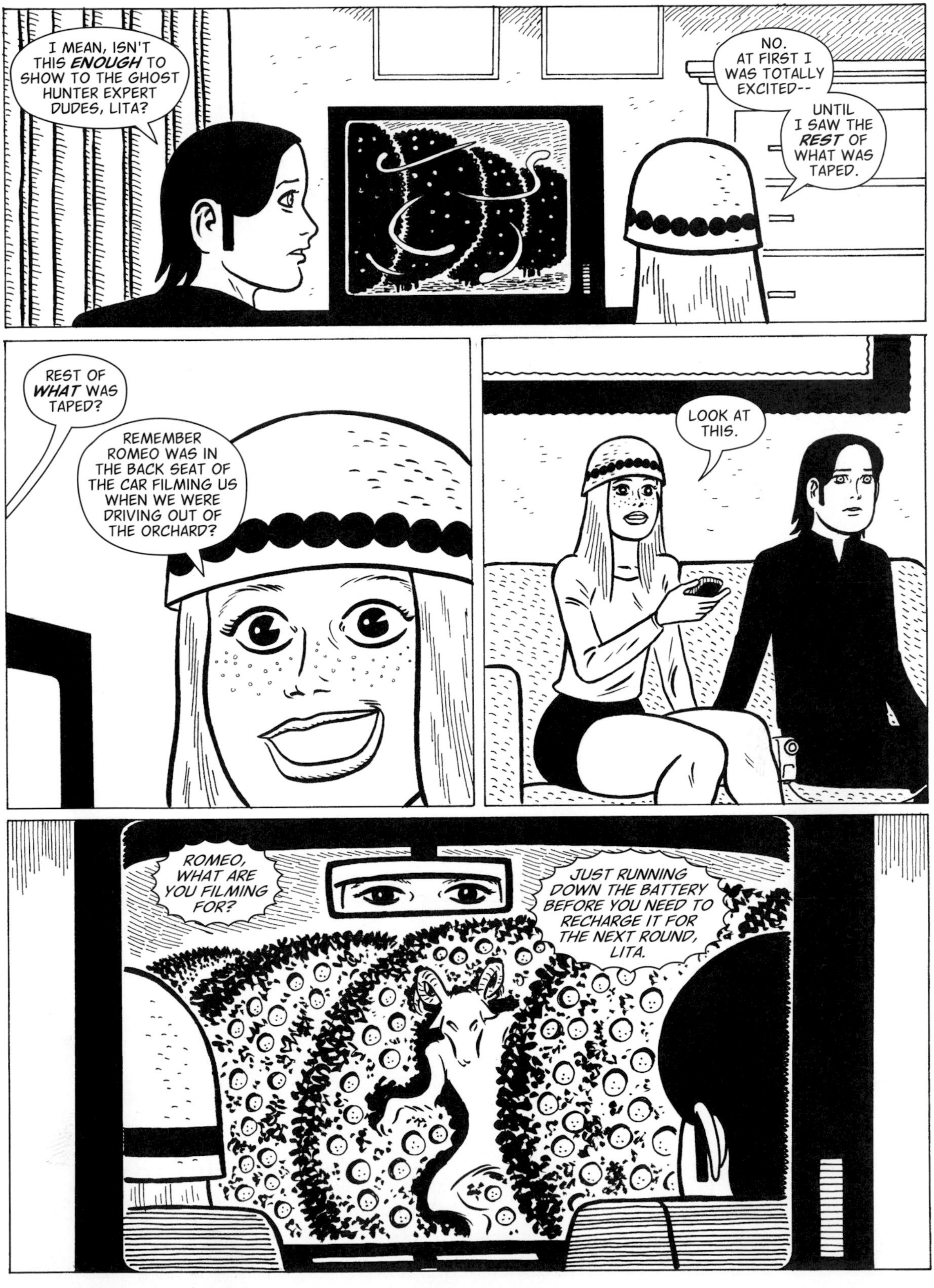
I MEAN, ISN'T THIS ENOUGH TO SHOW TO THE GHOST HUNTER EXPERT DUDES, LITA?
NO. AT FIRST I WAS TOTALLY EXCITED--
UNTIL I SAW THE REST OF WHAT WAS TAPED.
REST OF WHAT WAS TAPED?
REMEMBER ROMEO WAS IN THE BACK SEAT OF THE CAR FILMING US WHEN WE WERE DRIVING OUT OF THE ORCHARD?
LOOK AT THIS.
ROMEO, WHAT ARE YOU FILMING FOR?
JUST RUNNING DOWN THE BATTERY BEFORE YOU NEED TO RECHARGE IT FOR THE NEXT ROUND, LITA.

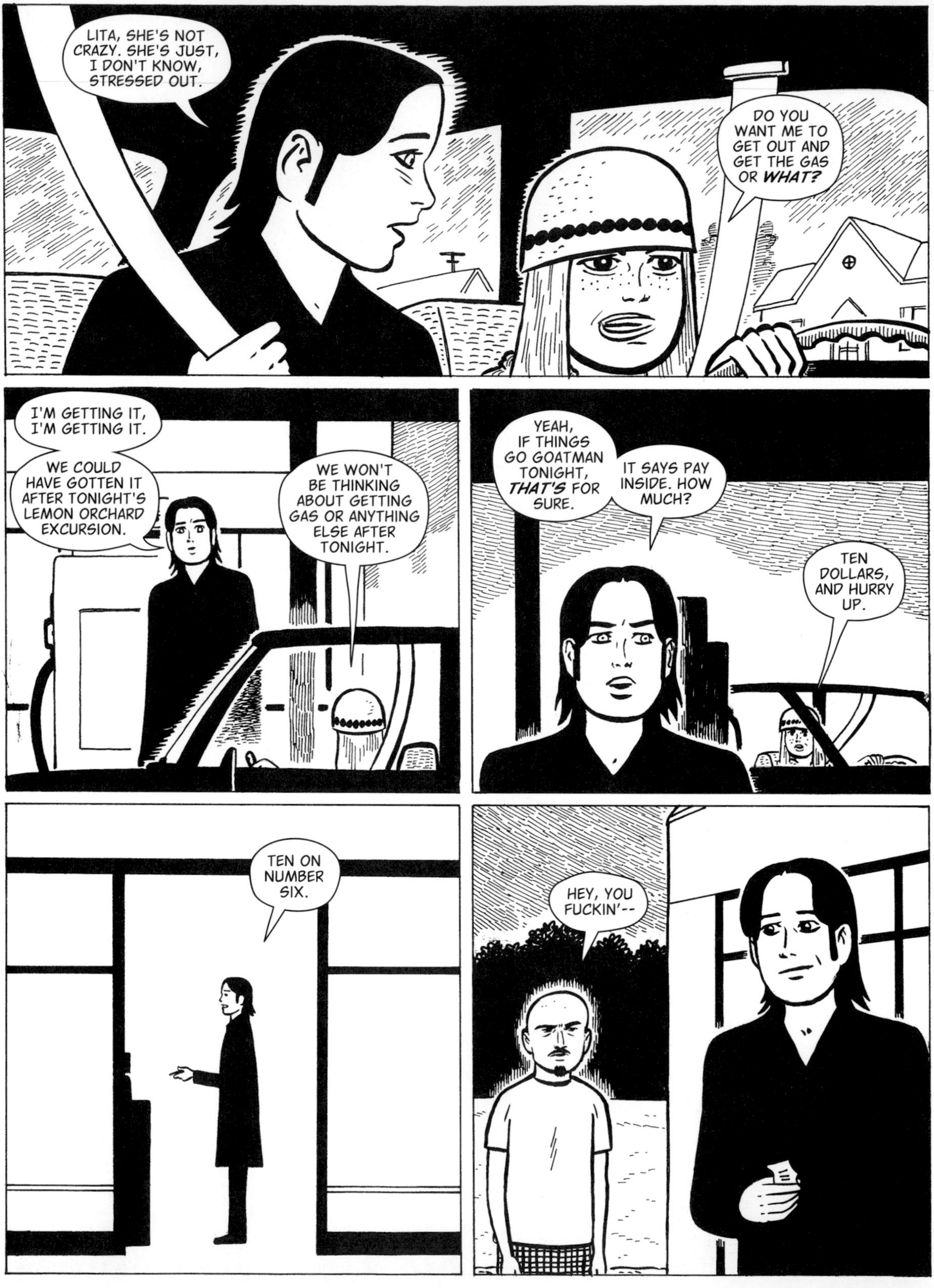

LITA, SHE'S NOT CRAZY. SHE'S JUST, I DON'T KNOW, STRESSED OUT.
DO YOU WANT ME TO GET OUT AND GET THE GAS OR WHAT?
I'M GETTING IT, I'M GETTING IT.
WE COULD HAVE GOTTEN IT AFTER TONIGHT'S LEMON ORCHARD EXCURSION.
WE WON'T BE THINKING ABOUT GETTING GAS OR ANYTHING ELSE AFTER TONIGHT.
YEAH, IF THINGS GO GOATMAN TONIGHT, THAT'S FOR SURE.
IT SAYS PAY INSIDE. HOW MUCH?
TEN DOLLARS, AND HURRY UP.
TEN ON NUMBER SIX.
HEY, YOU FUCKIN'--

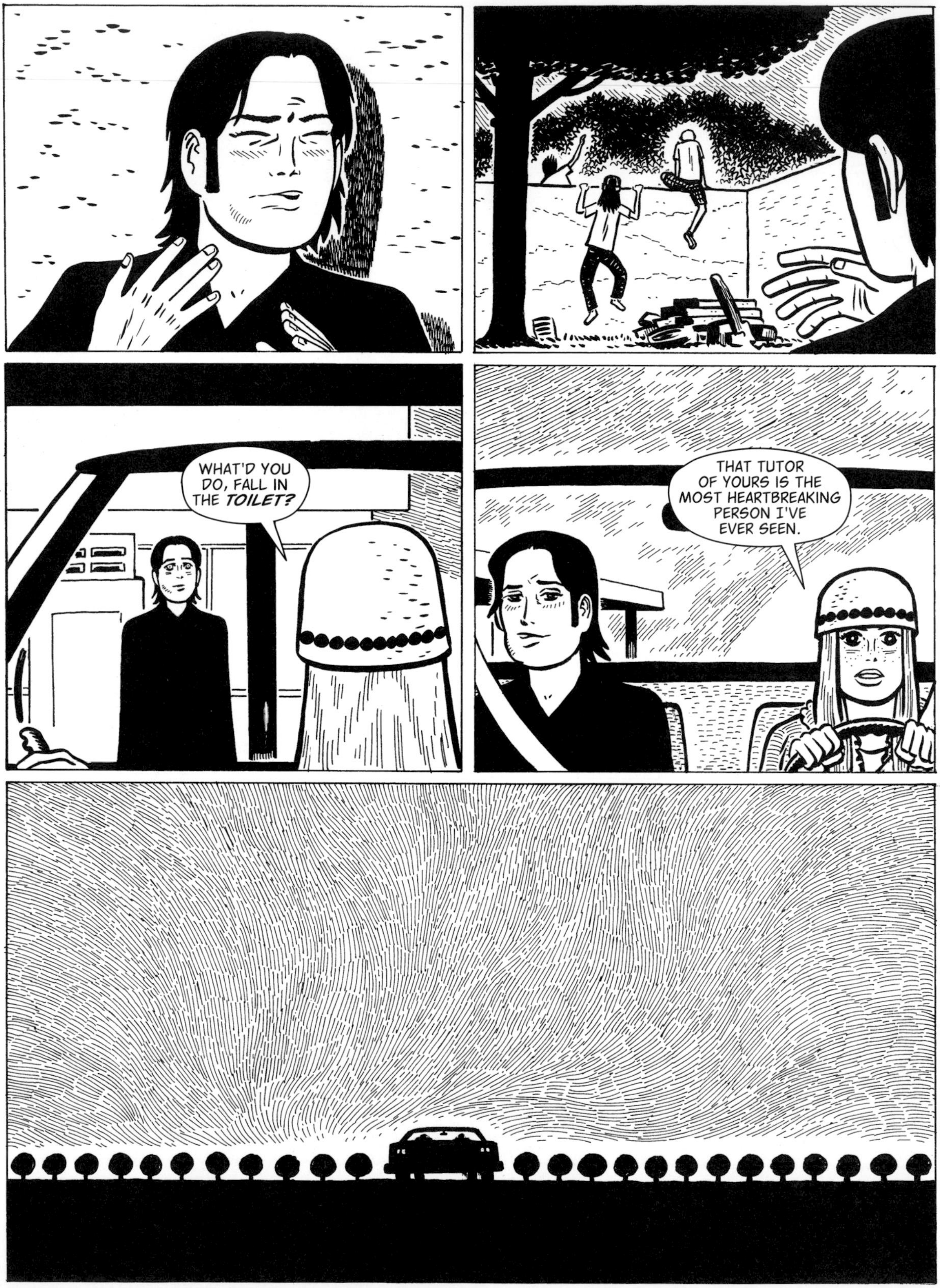
WHAT'D YOU DO, FALL IN THE *TOILET?*
THAT TUTOR OF YOURS IS THE MOST HEARTBREAKING PERSON I'VE EVER SEEN.

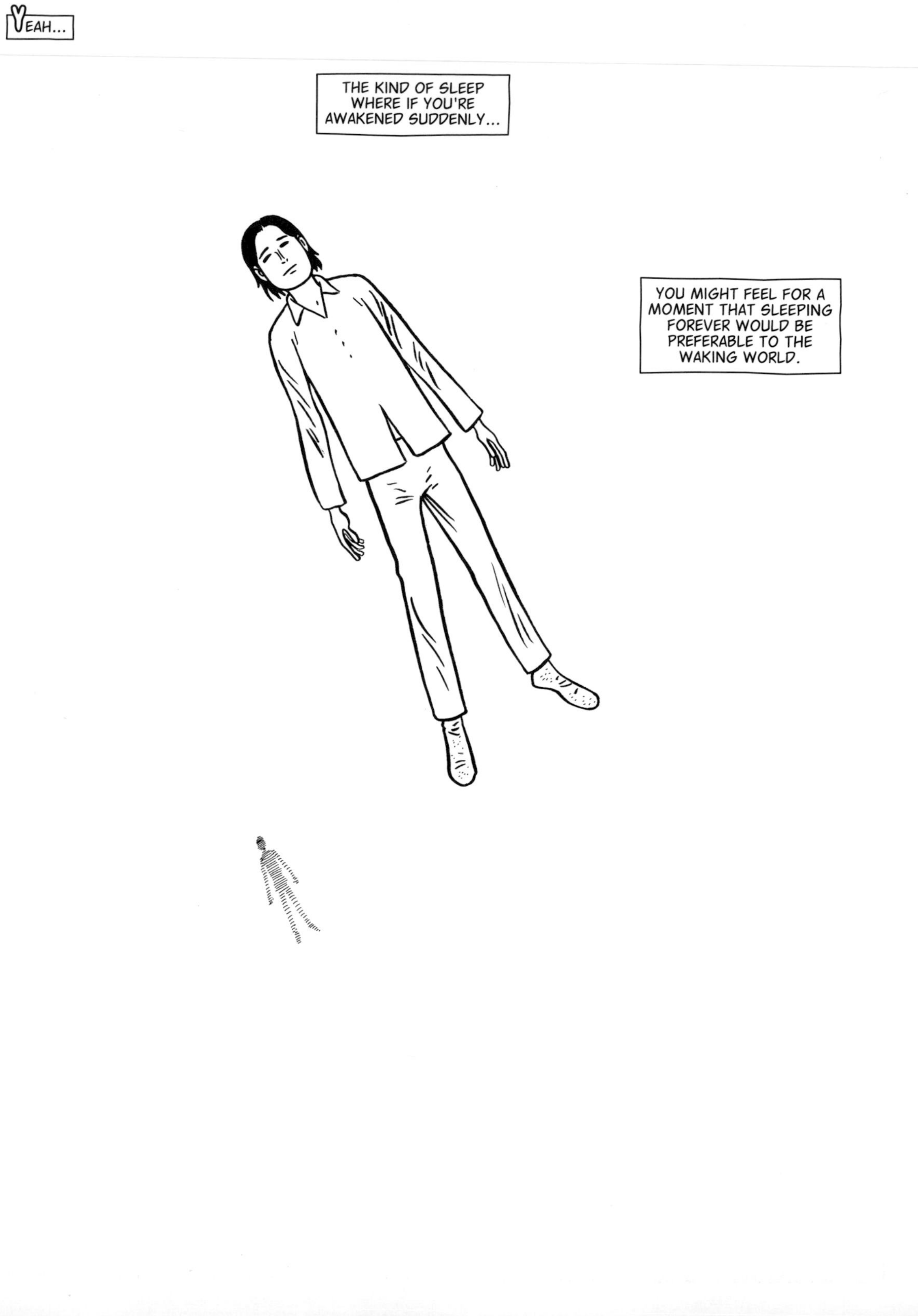
YEAH...
THE KIND OF SLEEP WHERE IF YOU'RE AWAKENED SUDDENLY...
YOU MIGHT FEEL FOR A MOMENT THAT SLEEPING FOREVER WOULD BE PREFERABLE TO THE WAKING WORLD.

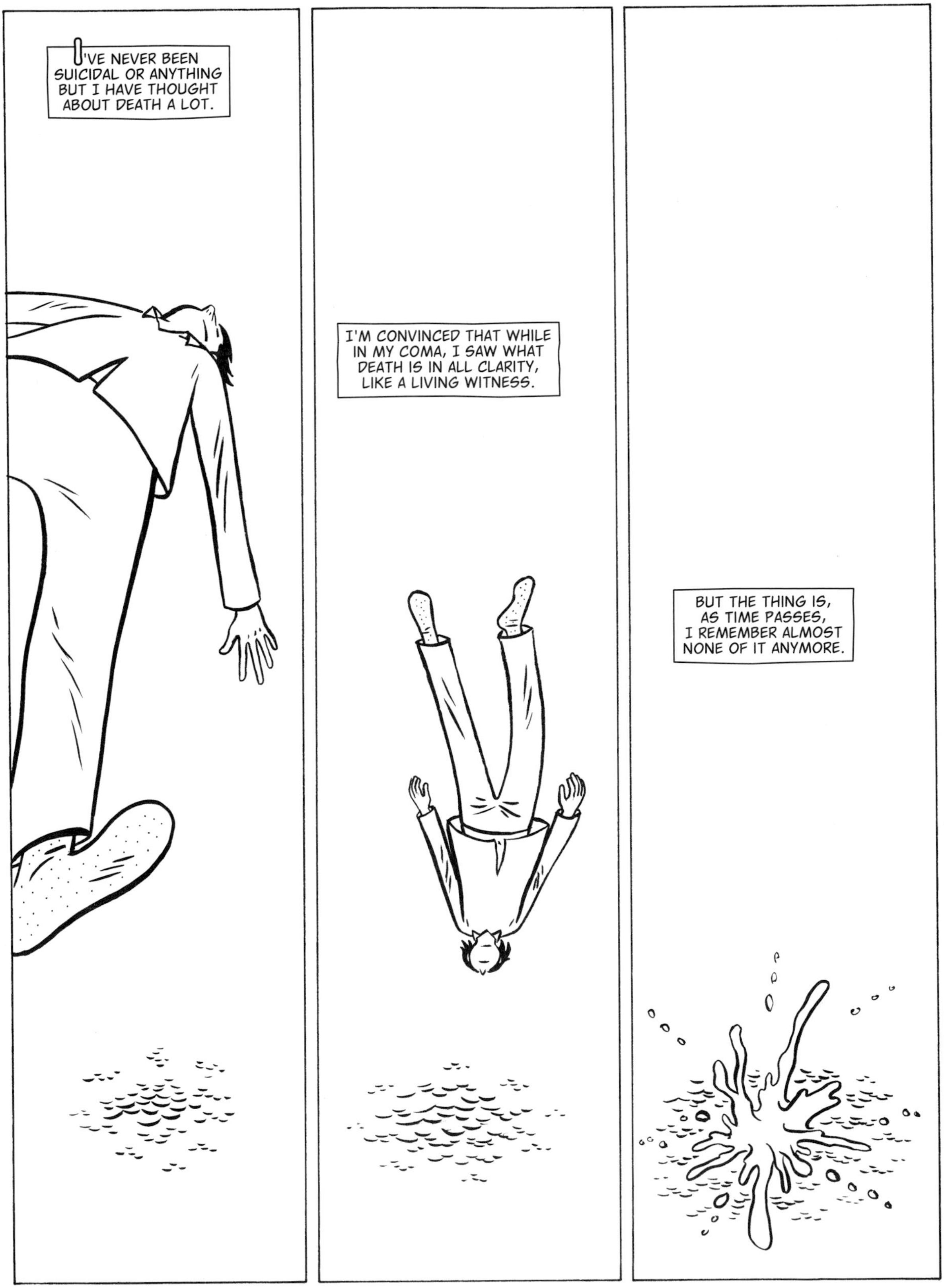
I'VE NEVER BEEN SUICIDAL OR ANYTHING BUT I HAVE THOUGHT ABOUT DEATH A LOT.
I'M CONVINCED THAT WHILE IN MY COMA, I SAW WHAT DEATH IS IN ALL CLARITY, LIKE A LIVING WITNESS.
BUT THE THING IS, AS TIME PASSES, I REMEMBER ALMOST NONE OF IT ANYMORE.

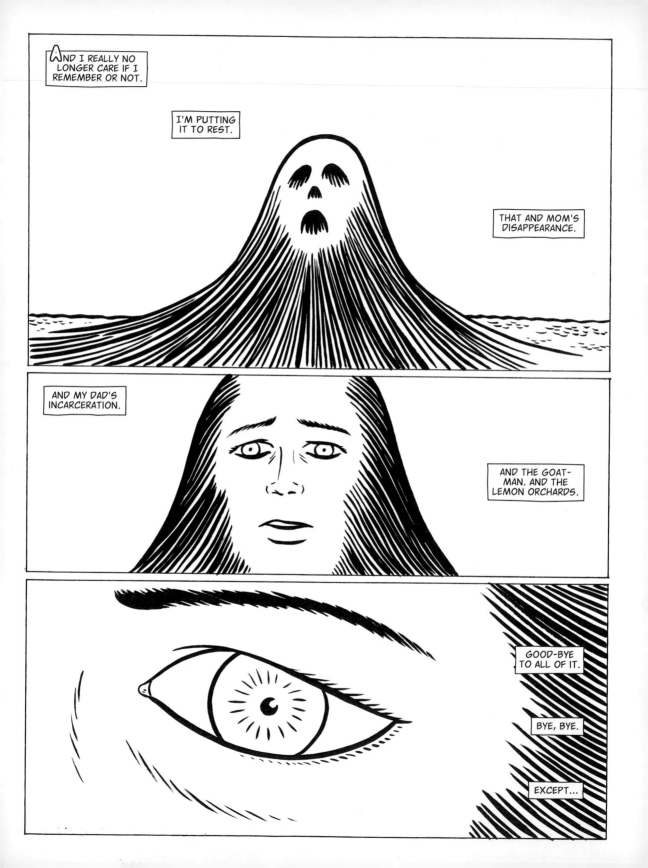

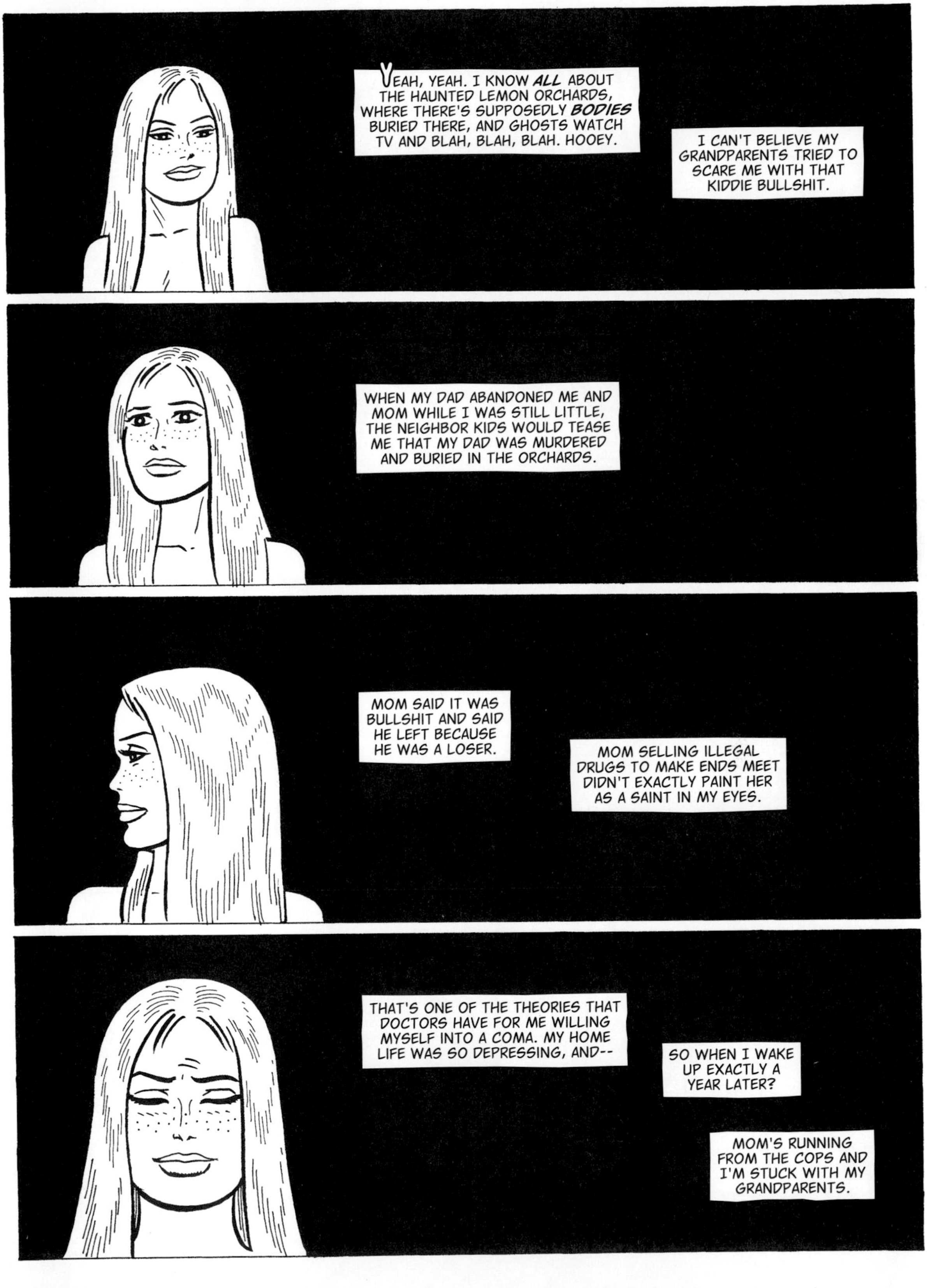
YEAH, YEAH. I KNOW ALL ABOUT THE HAUNTED LEMON ORCHARDS, WHERE THERE'S SUPPOSEDLY BODIES BURIED THERE, AND GHOSTS WATCH TV AND BLAH, BLAH, BLAH. HOOEY.
I CAN'T BELIEVE MY GRANDPARENTS TRIED TO SCARE ME WITH THAT KIDDIE BULLSHIT.
WHEN MY DAD ABANDONED ME AND MOM WHILE I WAS STILL LITTLE, THE NEIGHBOR KIDS WOULD TEASE ME THAT MY DAD WAS MURDERED AND BURIED IN THE ORCHARDS.
MOM SAID IT WAS BULLSHIT AND SAID HE LEFT BECAUSE HE WAS A LOSER.
MOM SELLING ILLEGAL DRUGS TO MAKE ENDS MEET DIDN'T EXACTLY PAINT HER AS A SAINT IN MY EYES.
THAT'S ONE OF THE THEORIES THAT DOCTORS HAVE FOR ME WILLING MYSELF INTO A COMA. MY HOME LIFE WAS SO DEPRESSING, AND--
SO WHEN I WAKE UP EXACTLY A YEAR LATER?
MOM'S RUNNING FROM THE COPS AND I'M STUCK WITH MY GRANDPARENTS.

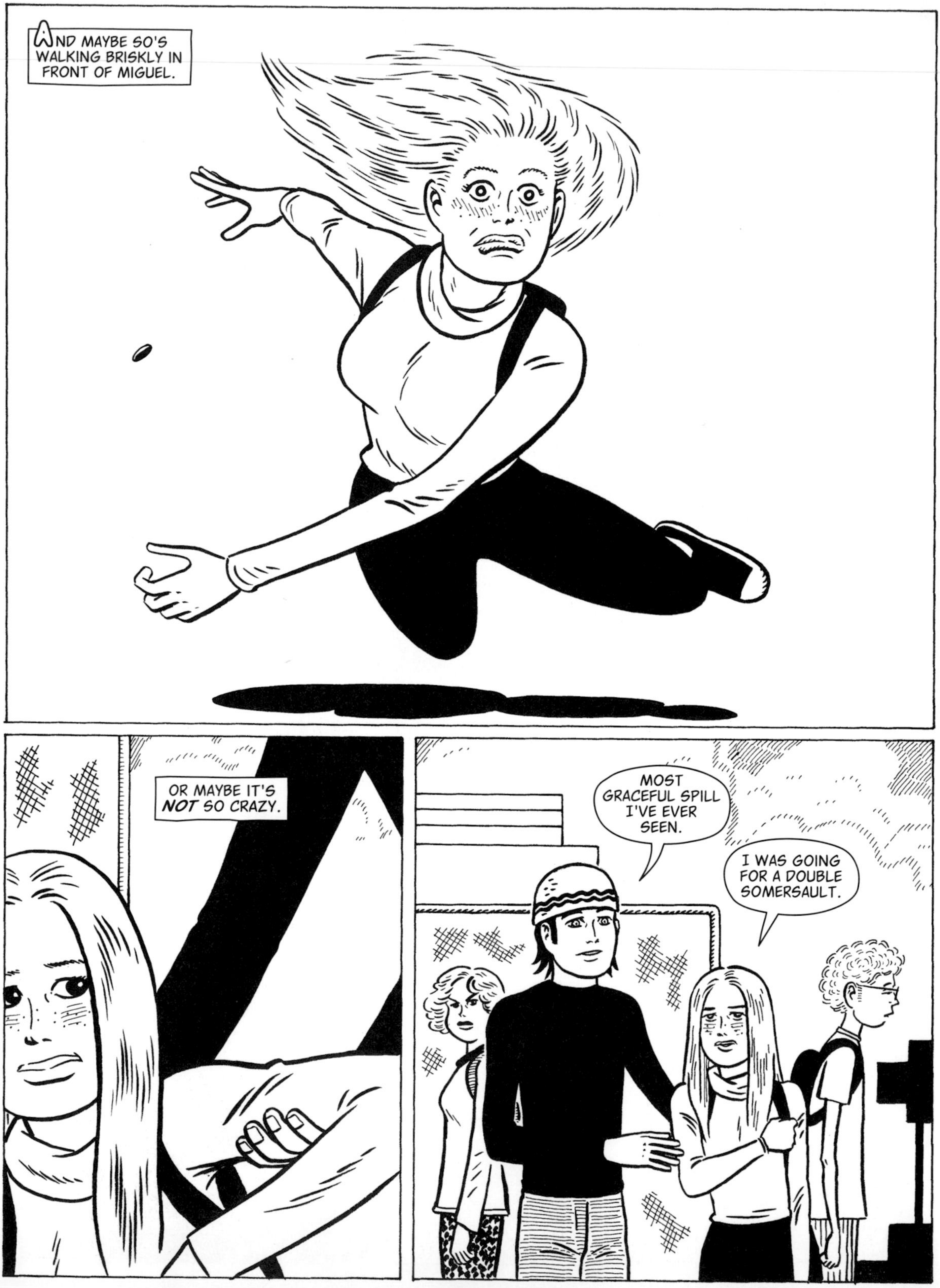
AND MAYBE SO'S WALKING BRISKLY IN FRONT OF MIGUEL.
OR MAYBE IT'S *NOT* SO CRAZY.
MOST GRACEFUL SPILL I'VE EVER SEEN.
I WAS GOING FOR A DOUBLE SOMERSAULT.

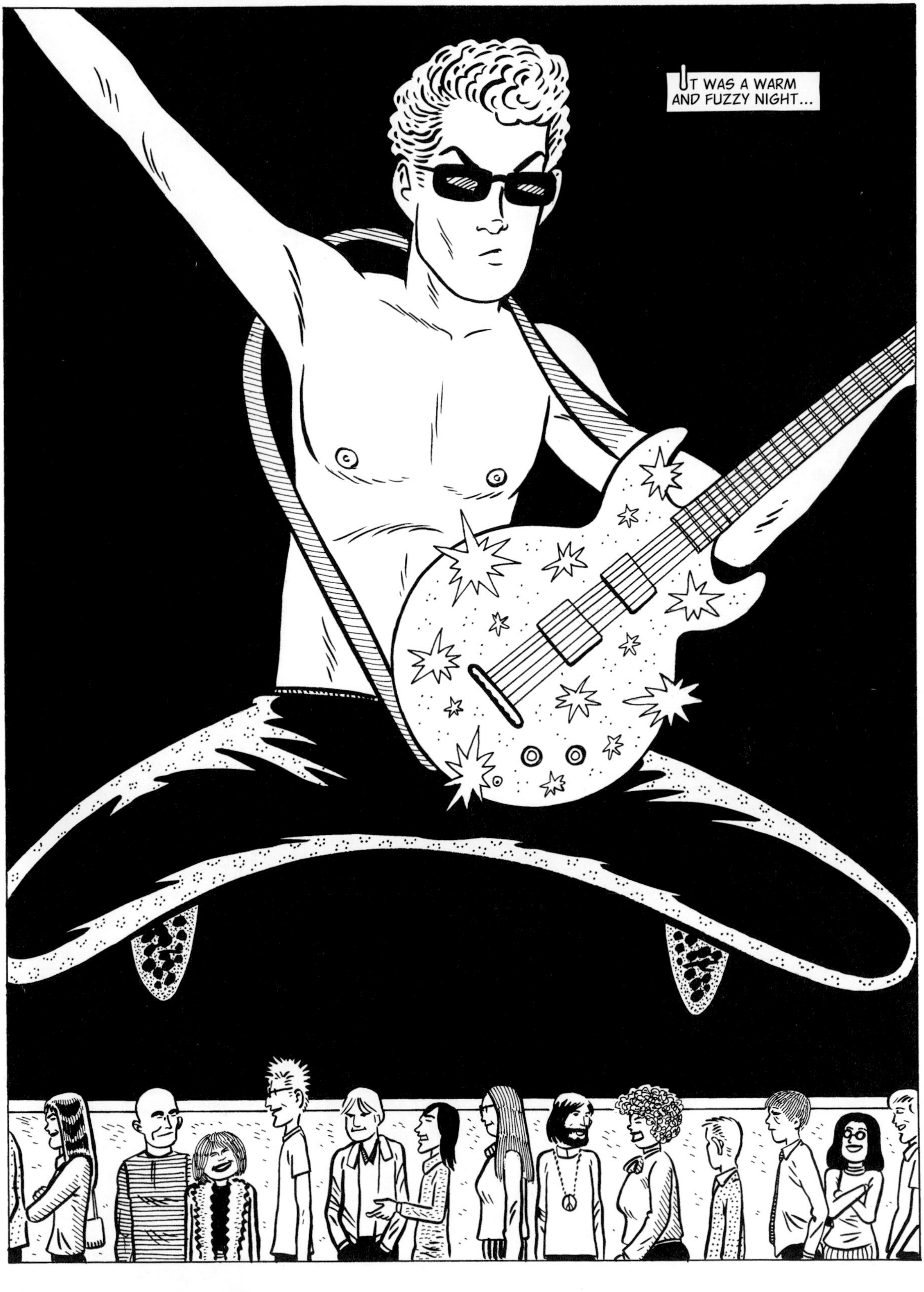
IT WAS A WARM AND FUZZY NIGHT...

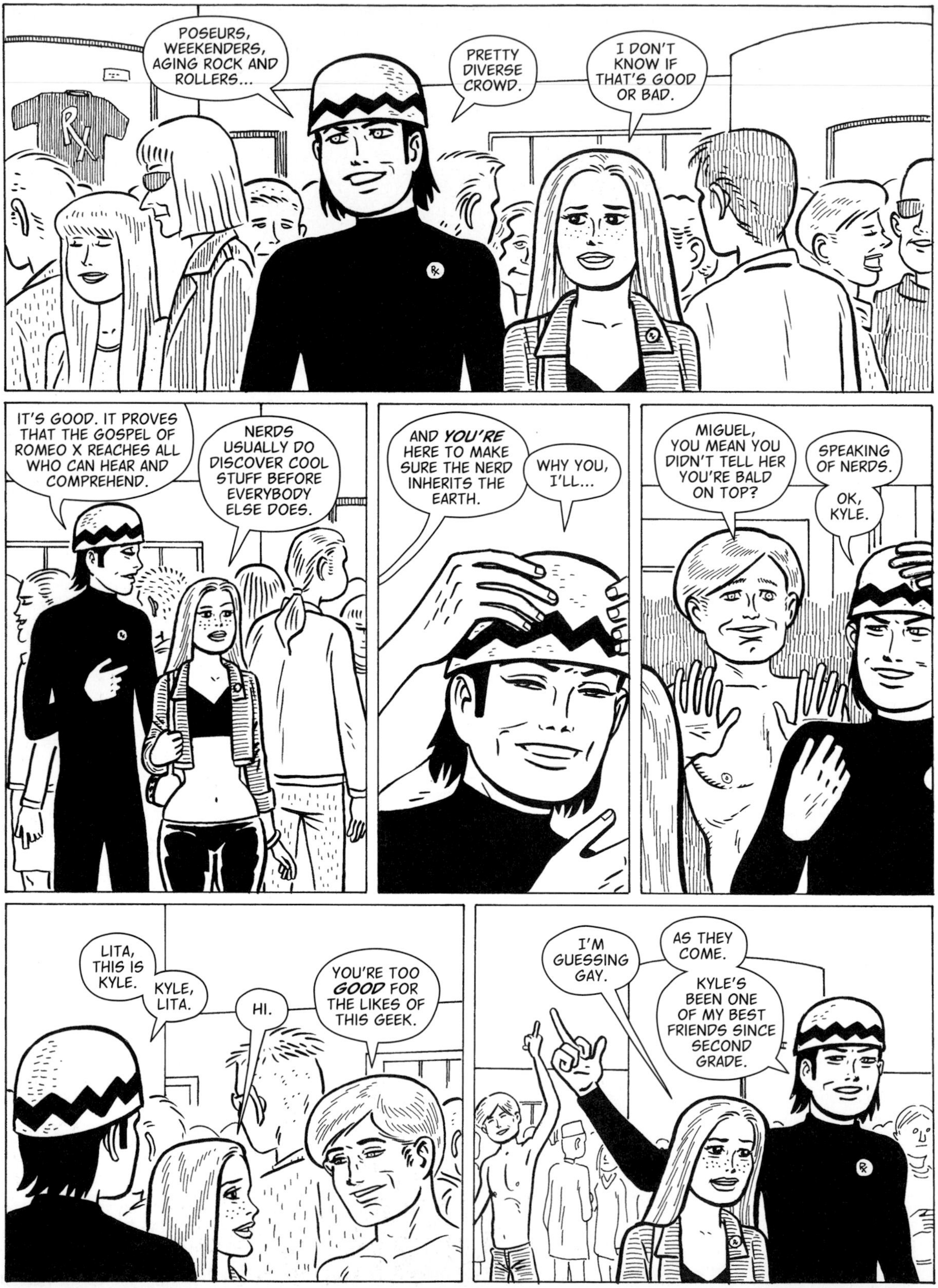
POSEURS, WEEKENDERS, AGING ROCK AND ROLLERS...
PRETTY DIVERSE CROWD.
I DON'T KNOW IF THAT'S GOOD OR BAD.
IT'S GOOD. IT PROVES THAT THE GOSPEL OF ROMEO X REACHES ALL WHO CAN HEAR AND COMPREHEND.
NERDS USUALLY DO DISCOVER COOL STUFF BEFORE EVERYBODY ELSE DOES.
AND YOU'RE HERE TO MAKE SURE THE NERD INHERITS THE EARTH.
WHY YOU, I'LL...
MIGUEL, YOU MEAN YOU DIDN'T TELL HER YOU'RE BALD ON TOP?
SPEAKING OF NERDS.
OK, KYLE.
LITA, THIS IS KYLE.
KYLE, LITA.
HI.
YOU'RE TOO GOOD FOR THE LIKES OF THIS GEEK.
I'M GUESSING GAY.
AS THEY COME.
KYLE'S BEEN ONE OF MY BEST FRIENDS SINCE SECOND GRADE.

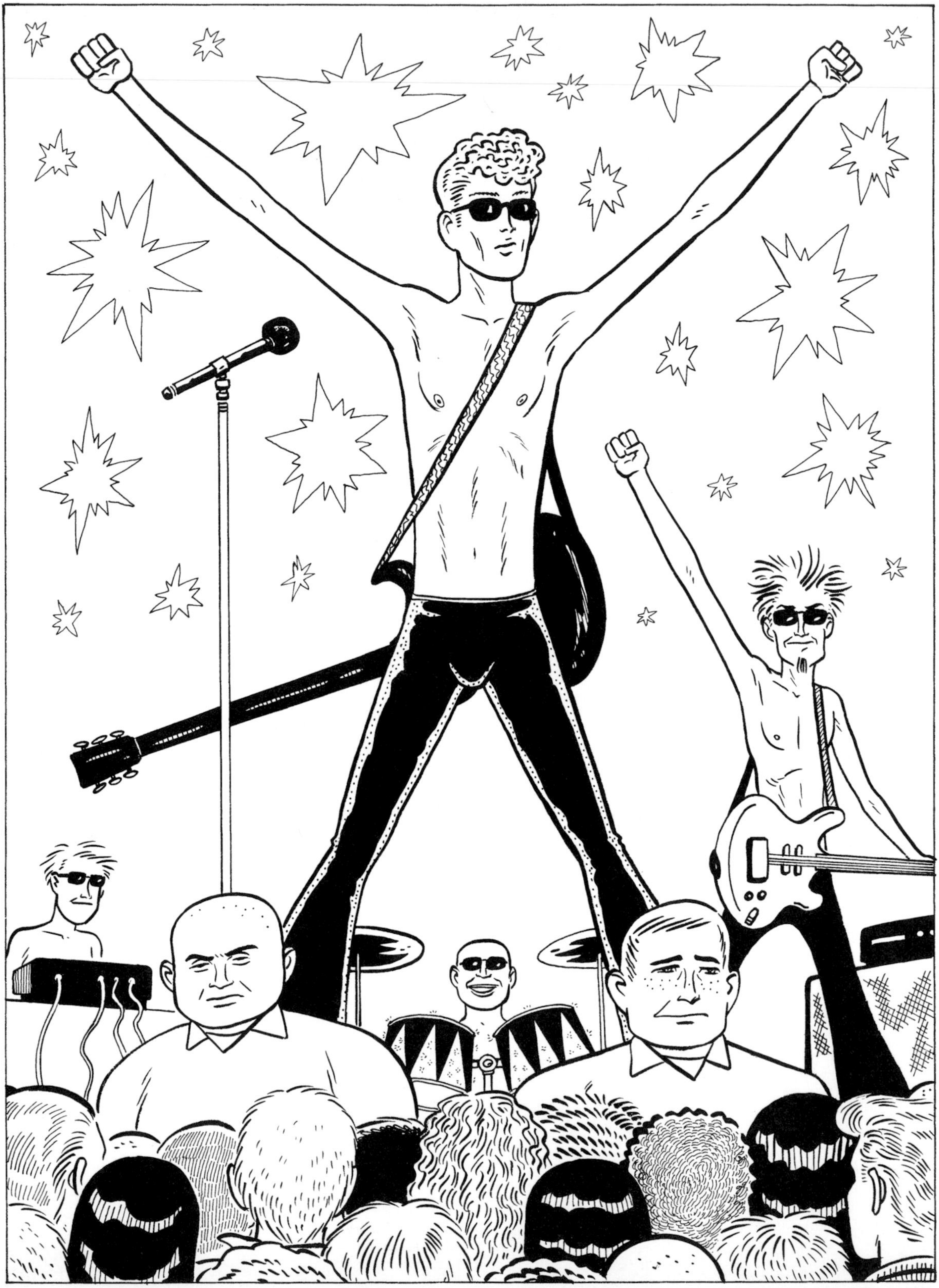

LOOKING AT THE MOON WITH THE TWO GUYS I WANT TO BE WITH MOST IN THE WHOLE WORLD.
A GIRL COULD GET USED TO THIS KIND OF THING.

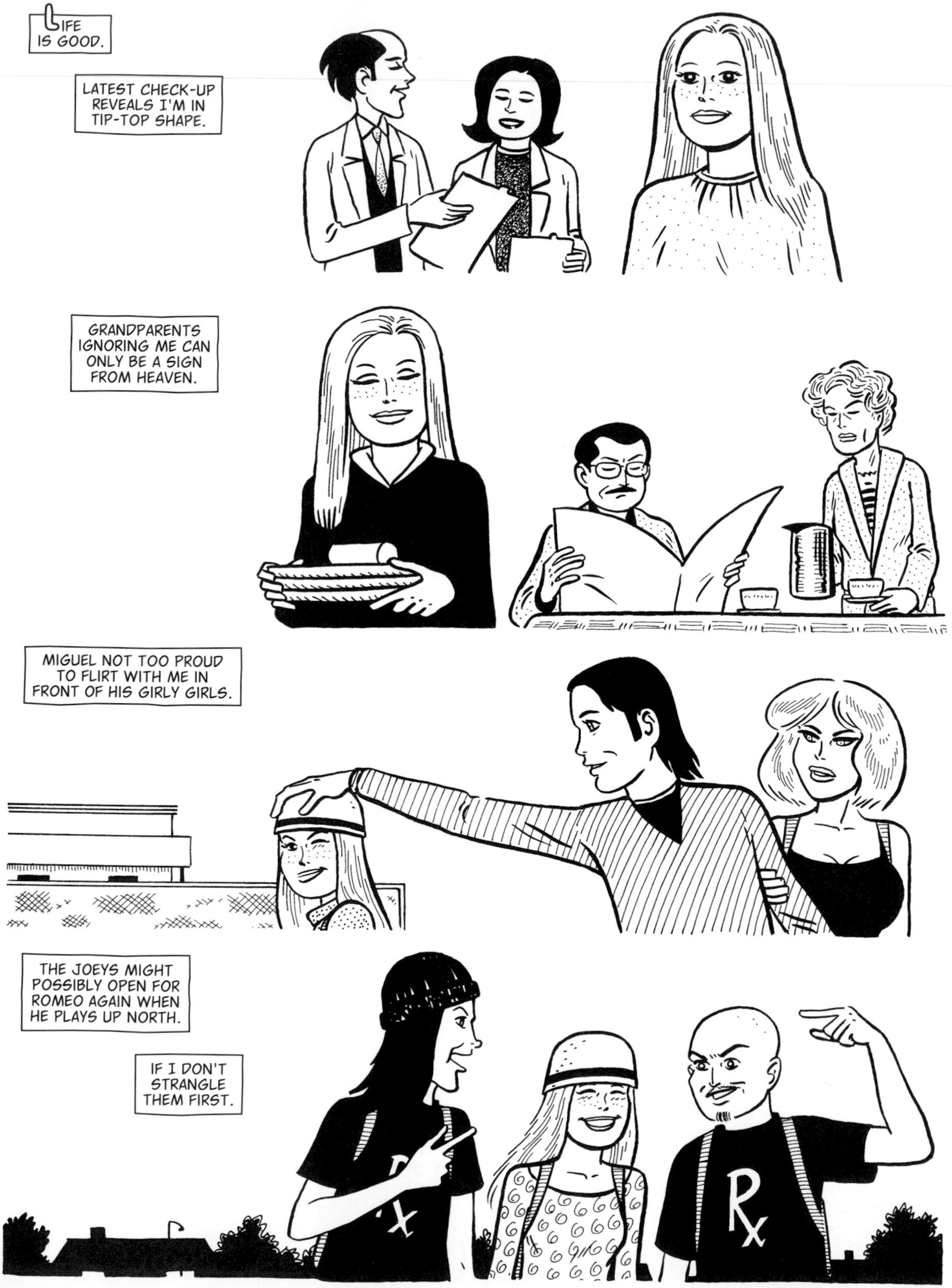
LIFE IS GOOD.
LATEST CHECK-UP REVEALS I'M IN TIP-TOP SHAPE.
GRANDPARENTS IGNORING ME CAN ONLY BE A SIGN FROM HEAVEN.
MIGUEL NOT TOO PROUD TO FLIRT WITH ME IN FRONT OF HIS GIRLY GIRLS.
THE JOEYS MIGHT POSSIBLY OPEN FOR ROMEO AGAIN WHEN HE PLAYS UP NORTH.
IF I DON'T STRANGLE THEM FIRST.
Rx

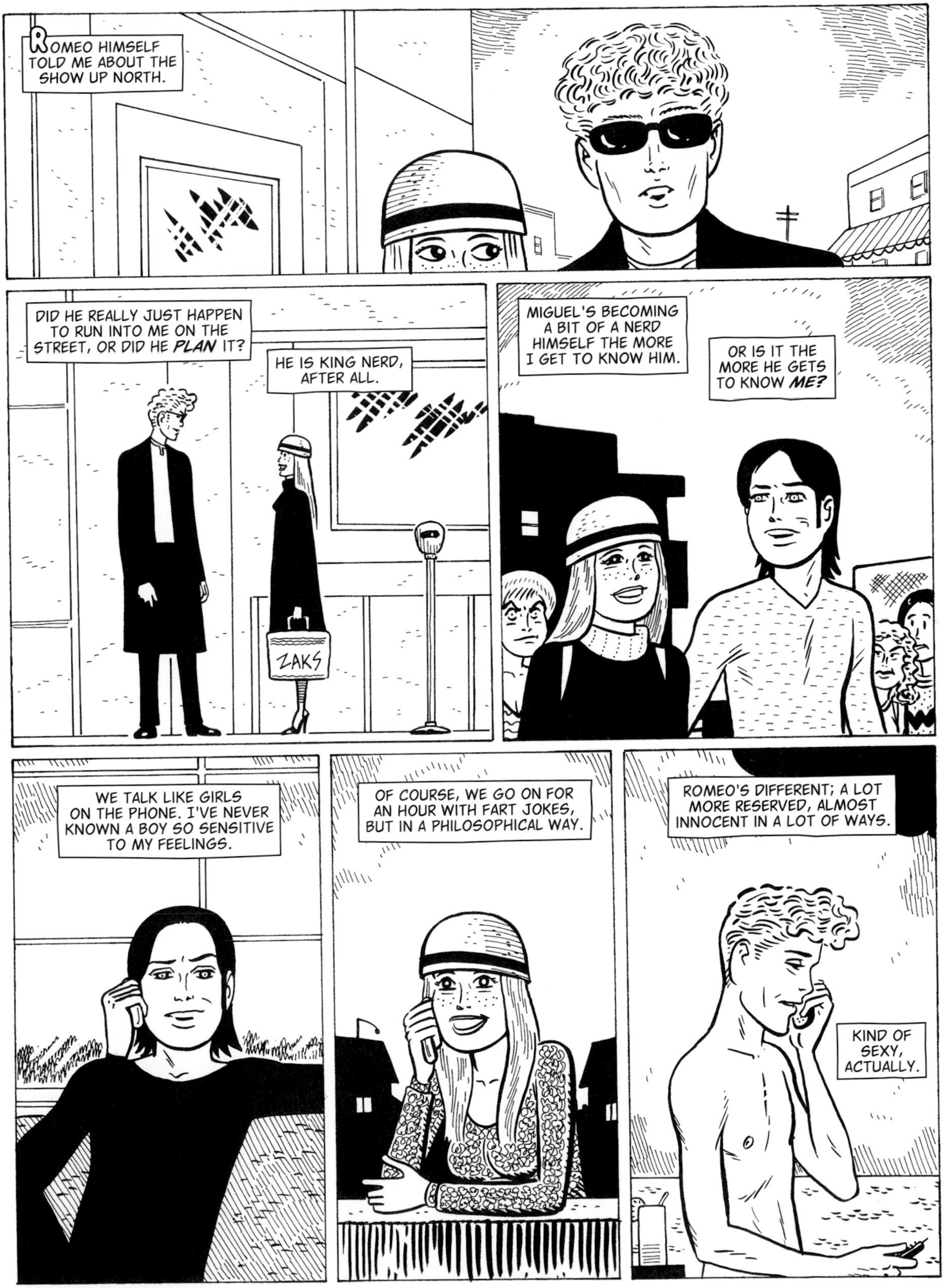
ROMEO HIMSELF TOLD ME ABOUT THE SHOW UP NORTH.
DID HE REALLY JUST HAPPEN TO RUN INTO ME ON THE STREET, OR DID HE *PLAN* IT?
HE IS KING NERD, AFTER ALL.
ZAKS
MIGUEL'S BECOMING A BIT OF A NERD HIMSELF THE MORE I GET TO KNOW HIM.
OR IS IT THE MORE HE GETS TO KNOW *ME?*
WE TALK LIKE GIRLS ON THE PHONE. I'VE NEVER KNOWN A BOY SO SENSITIVE TO MY FEELINGS.
OF COURSE, WE GO ON FOR AN HOUR WITH FART JOKES, BUT IN A PHILOSOPHICAL WAY.
ROMEO'S DIFFERENT; A LOT MORE RESERVED, ALMOST INNOCENT IN A LOT OF WAYS.
KIND OF SEXY, ACTUALLY.

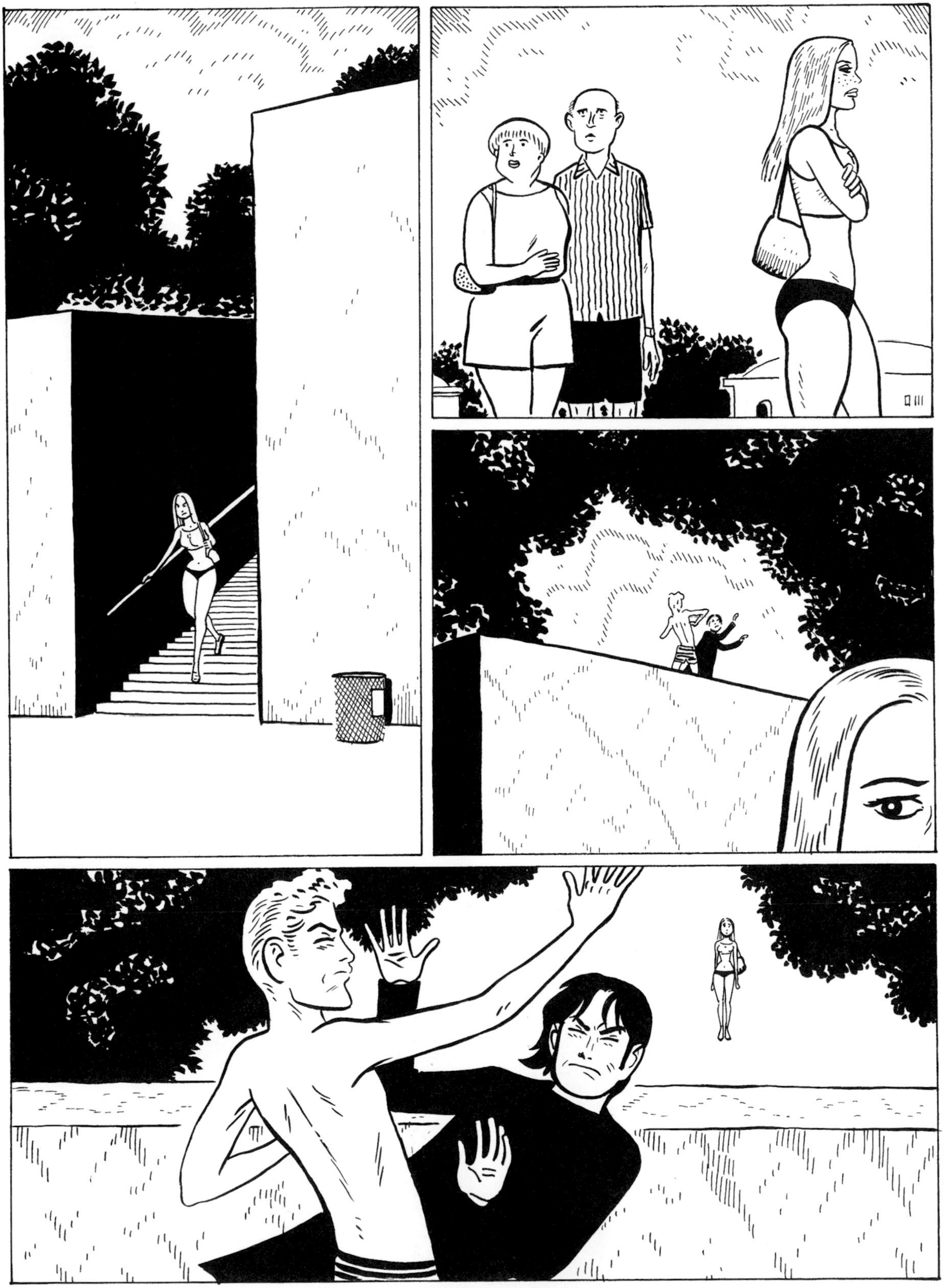

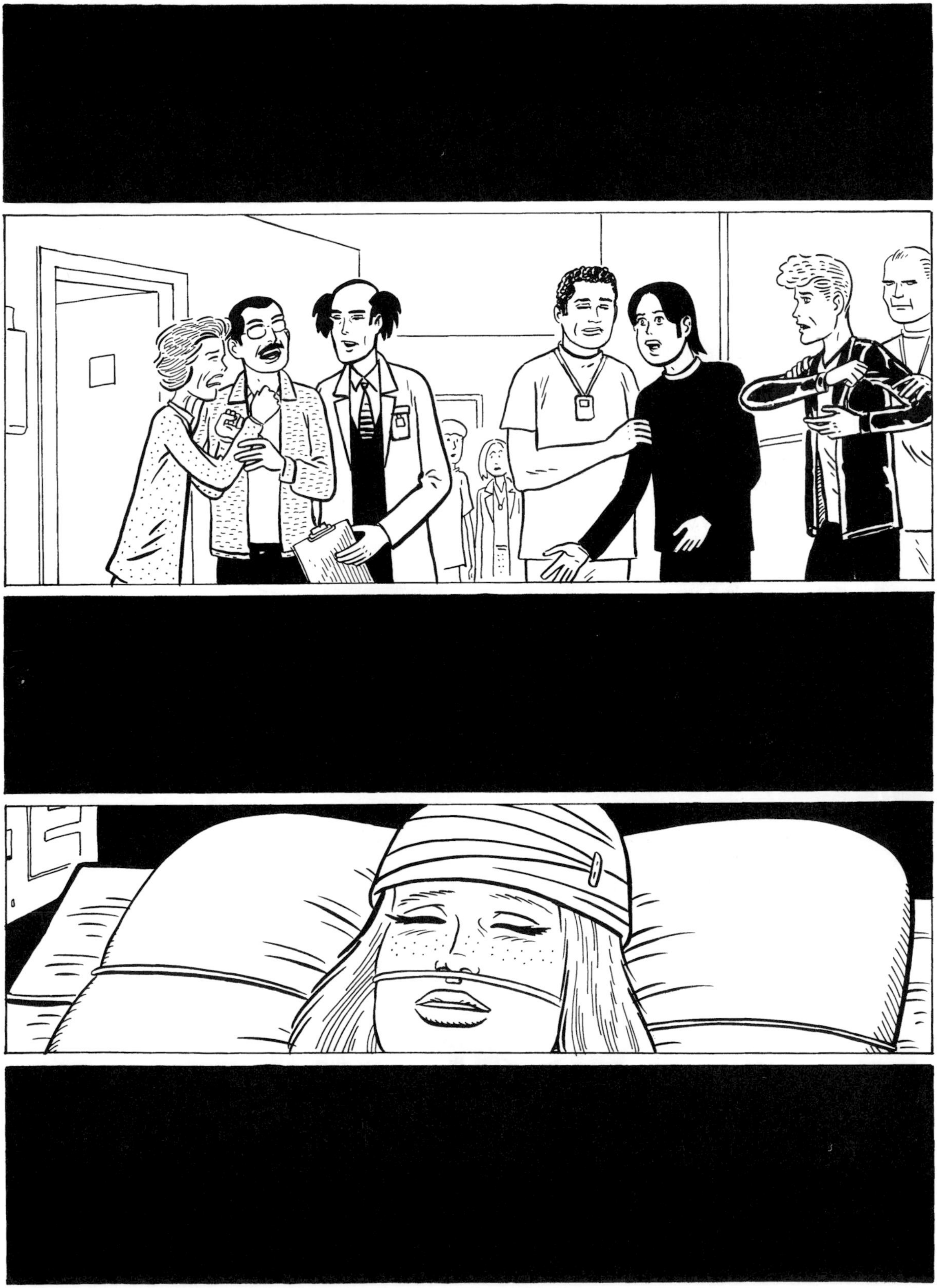

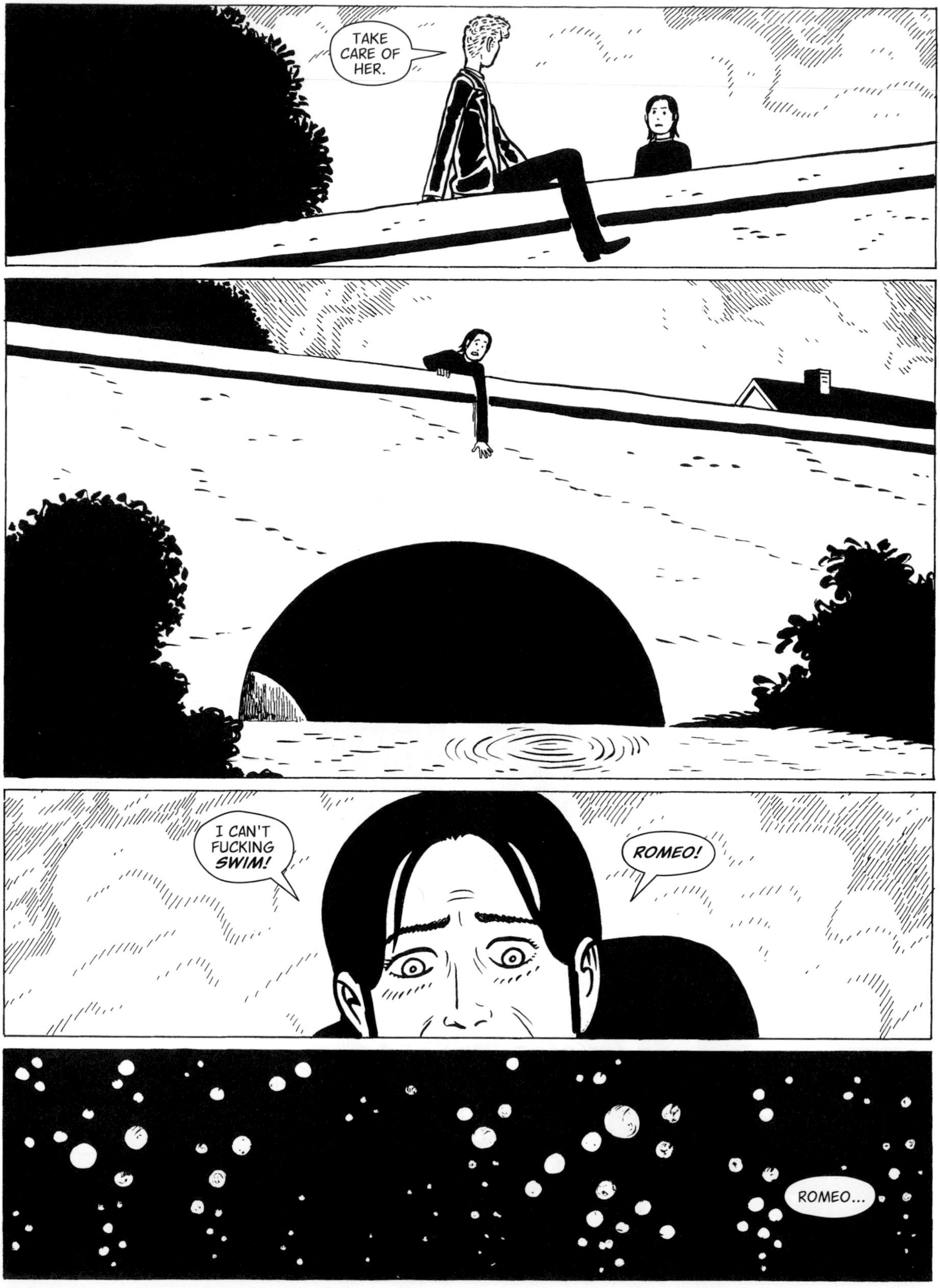
TAKE CARE OF HER.
I CAN'T FUCKING SWIM!
ROMEO!
ROMEO...

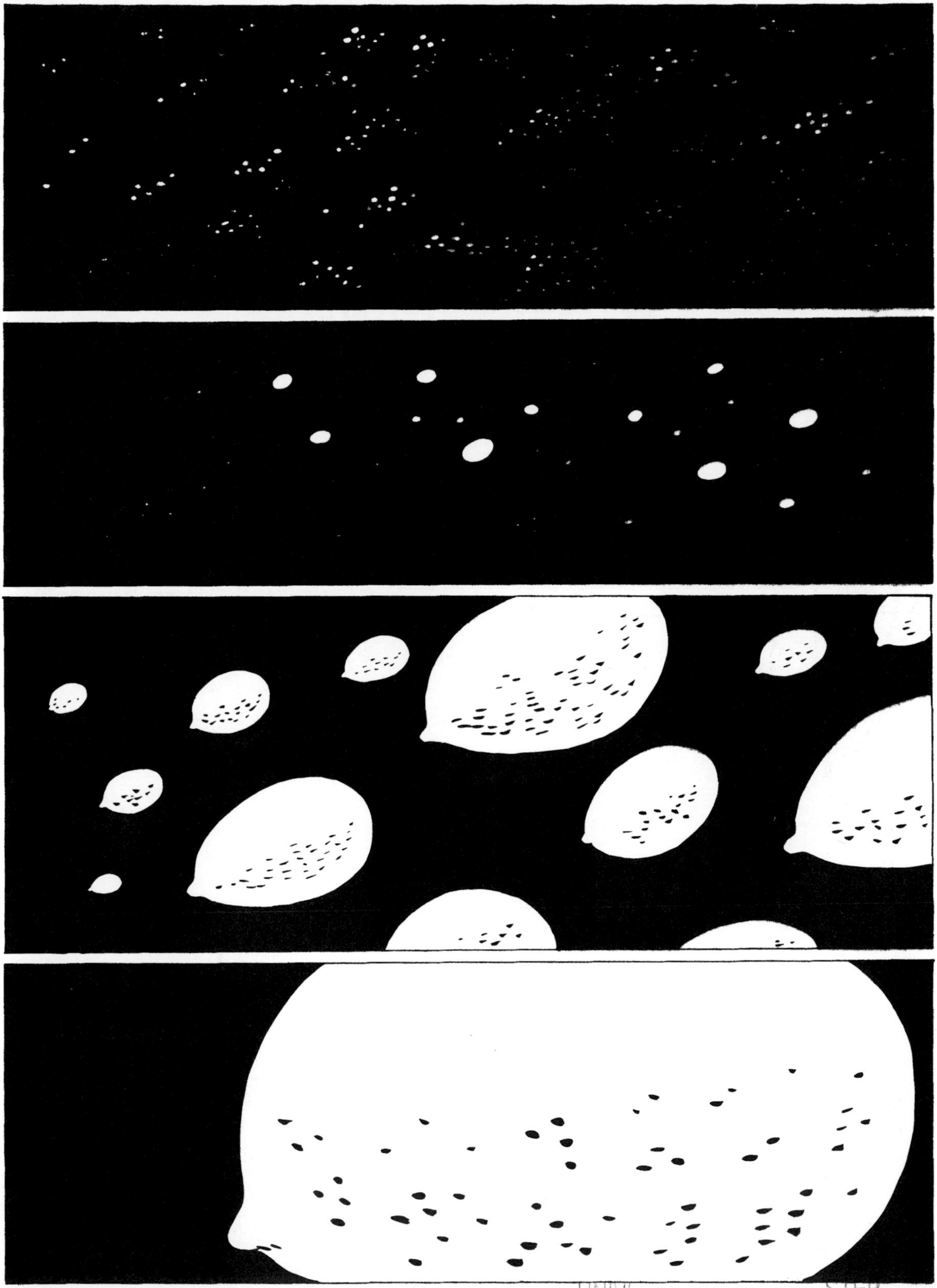

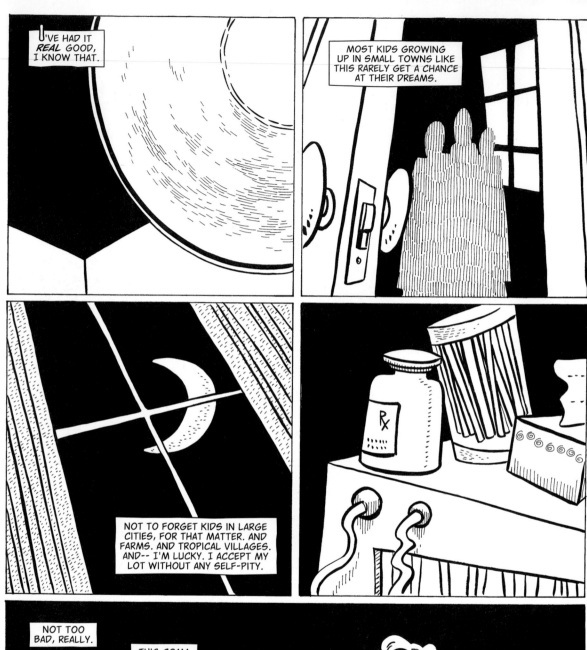

I'VE HAD IT *REAL* GOOD, I KNOW THAT.

MOST KIDS GROWING UP IN SMALL TOWNS LIKE THIS RARELY GET A CHANCE AT THEIR DREAMS.

NOT TO FORGET KIDS IN LARGE CITIES, FOR THAT MATTER. AND FARMS. AND TROPICAL VILLAGES. AND-- I'M LUCKY. I ACCEPT MY LOT WITHOUT ANY SELF-PITY.

NOT TOO BAD, REALLY.

THIS COMA BIT, I MEAN.

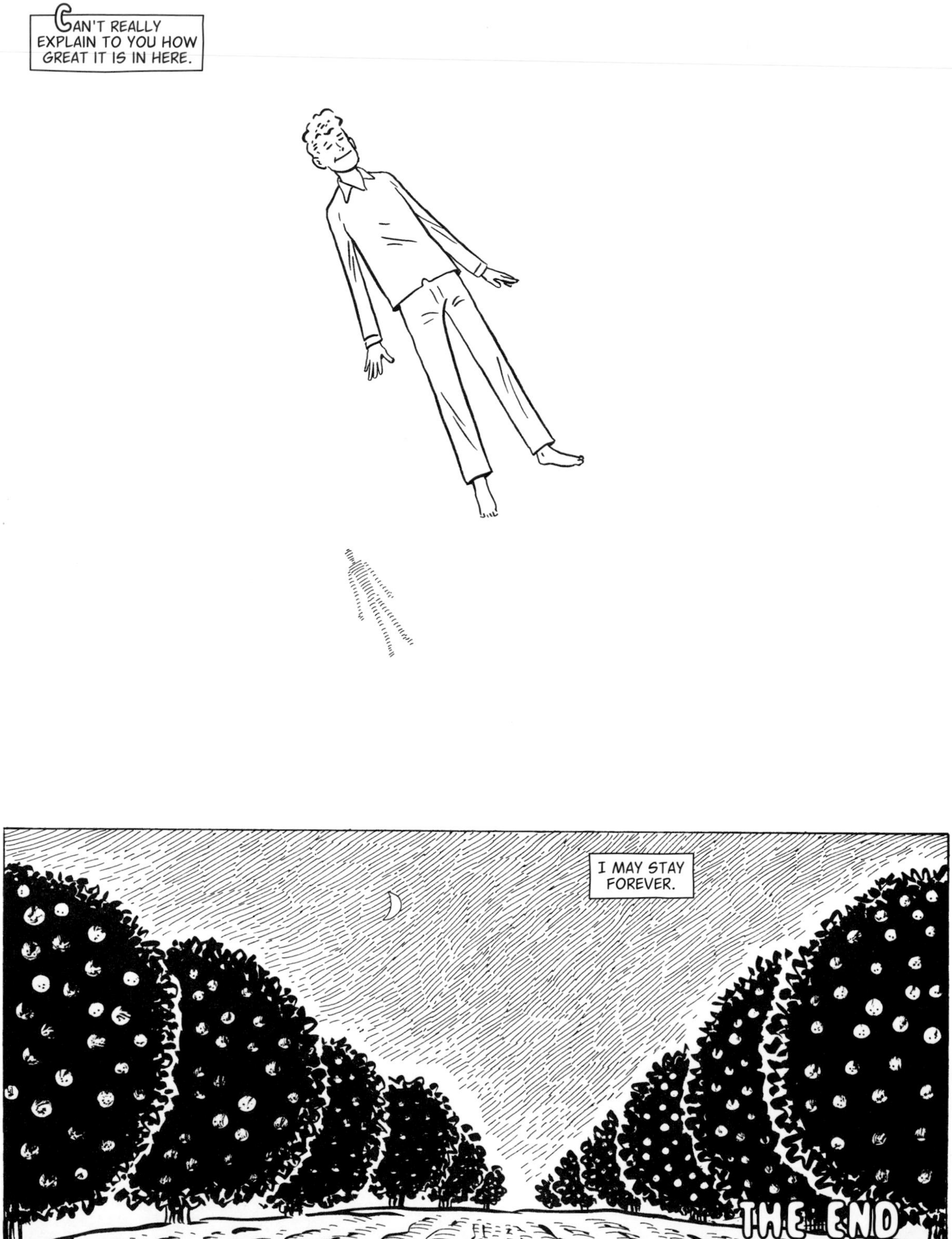
CAN'T REALLY EXPLAIN TO YOU HOW GREAT IT IS IN HERE.
I MAY STAY FOREVER.
THE END

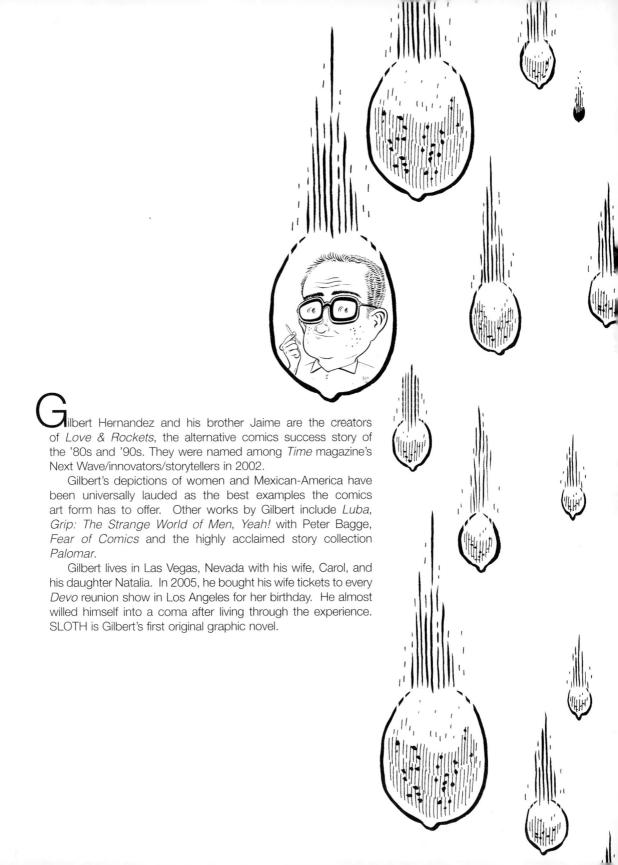

Gilbert Hernandez and his brother Jaime are the creators of *Love & Rockets*, the alternative comics success story of the '80s and '90s. They were named among *Time* magazine's Next Wave/innovators/storytellers in 2002.

Gilbert's depictions of women and Mexican-America have been universally lauded as the best examples the comics art form has to offer. Other works by Gilbert include *Luba*, *Grip: The Strange World of Men*, *Yeah!* with Peter Bagge, *Fear of Comics* and the highly acclaimed story collection *Palomar*.

Gilbert lives in Las Vegas, Nevada with his wife, Carol, and his daughter Natalia. In 2005, he bought his wife tickets to every *Devo* reunion show in Los Angeles for her birthday. He almost willed himself into a coma after living through the experience. SLOTH is Gilbert's first original graphic novel.

Look for these other VERTIGO books:

100 BULLETS
Brian Azzarello/Eduardo Risso

With one special briefcase, Agent Graves gives you the chance
to kill without retribution. But what is the real price
for this chance — and who is setting it?

DOOM PATROL
Grant Morrison/Richard Case/
John Nyberg/Doug Braithwaite/various

The World's Strangest Heroes are reimagined as even stranger
and more otherworldly in this groundbreaking series
exploring the mysteries of identity and madness.

FABLES
Bill Willingham/Lan Medina/
Mark Buckingham/Steve Leialoha

The immortal characters of popular fairy tales have been
driven from their homelands and now live hidden among us,
trying to cope with life in 21st-century Manhattan.

LUCIFER
Mike Carey/Peter Gross/Scott Hampton/
Chris Weston/Dean Ormston/various

Walking out of Hell (and out of the pages of THE SANDMAN),
an ambitious Lucifer Morningstar creates a new cosmos
modelled after his own image.

PREACHER
Garth Ennis/Steve Dillon/various

This modern American epic of life, death, God, love, and redemption
is loaded to the brim with sex, booze, and blood.

THE SANDMAN
Neil Gaiman/various

The New York Times best-selling author blends modern myth,
historical legend and dark fantasy in one of the most
acclaimed and celebrated comics titles ever published.

TRANSMETROPOLITAN
Warren Ellis/Darick Robertson/various

This exuberant trip into a frenetic future stars an outlaw
journalist named Spider Jerusalem who battles hypocrisy,
corruption, and sobriety.

Y: THE LAST MAN
Brian K. Vaughan/Pia Guerra/José Marzán, Jr.

An unexplained plague kills every male mammal on Earth —
all except Yorick Brown and his pet monkey. Will he survive this
new, emasculated world to discover what killed his fellow men?

HEAVY LIQUID
Paul Pope

A mysterious man known as "S" is on a quest for Heavy Liquid —
which is at once a drug and an art form.

100%
Paul Pope

Four love-crossed strangers collide in futuristic Manhattan.

THE ORIGINALS
Dave Gibbons

For two childhood friends, there's nothing more important than
belonging to the Originals. But being a part of the "in" crowd
brings its own deadly consequences.

THE QUITTER
Harvey Pekar/Dean Haspiel

The creator of *American Splendor* reveals his troubled
teen years as the neighborhood bully.

CAN'T GET NO
Rick Veitch

A daringly poetic exploration of one man's spiritual
road trip across America in the wake of 9-11.

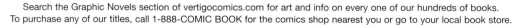